D1034893

Women Beware Women

THE NEW MERMAIDS

General Editors
PHILIP BROCKBANK
Professor of English, York University

BRIAN MORRIS
Senior Lecturer in English, York University

Women Beware Women

THOMAS MIDDLETON

Edited by ROMA GILL

ERNEST BENN LIMITED
LONDON

First published in this form 1968
by Ernest Benn Limited
Bouverie House · *Fleet Street* · *London* · *EC4*
© Ernest Benn Limited 1968
Distributed in Canada by
The General *Publishing Company Limited* · **Toronto**
Printed in Great Britain

510-34161-6

TO
JOHN KIRKHAM

CONTENTS

ACKNOWLEDGEMENTS

I SHOULD LIKE to thank Mark Roberts, who translated Malespini for me; and the University of Sheffield, which gave me a grant from its Research Fund.

ROMA GILL

ABBREVIATIONS

THE FOLLOWING abbreviations have been used in the notes:

O   The first (octavo) edition of *Women Beware Women.*

Bullen   *The Works of Thomas Middleton*, ed. A. H. Bullen (1885–6).

Dyce   *The Works of Thomas Middleton*, ed. Alexander Dyce (1840).

Hipolito &   *The True History of the Tragicke Loves of Hipolito*
Isabella   *and Isabella* (1628).

Moryson 4 *Shakespeare's Europe* (Part IV of Fynes Moryson's *Itinerary*), ed. Charles Hughes (1903).

Mulryne   *Women Beware Women*, ed. J. R. Mulryne (unpublished thesis, Cambridge, 1962).

Simpson   'Thomas Middleton's *Women Beware Women*', by Percy Simpson, *Modern Language Review* XXXIII (1938).

Tilley   *A Dictionary of the Proverbs in England in the Sixteenth and Seventeenth Centuries*, ed. M. P. Tilley (Ann Arbor, 1950).

INTRODUCTION

THE AUTHOR

THE SON OF a London bricklayer, Thomas Middleton was born in April 1580. Six years later his father died, leaving the family some reasonable financial comfort. This brought Mrs Middleton, who rashly re-married within the year, a life of quarrels and litigation with her second husband, but her son's share of the estate allowed him an Oxford education. He may himself have been the poor scholar he describes in *Father Hubburd's Tales*, one who 'conversed with midnight' before he was 'led to the lickerish study of poetry, that sweet honey-poison, that swells a supple scholar with unprofitableness and delicious false conceits'.[1] In 1601 he sold his property to his brother-in-law to pay for 'maintenance with meat drinke and apparrell' and for 'advancement & preferment in the University of Oxford'. By this time, however, he had left the university and was reported to be in London, 'daylie accompaninge the players'; soon he was married to the sister of one of them.

Middleton, like many other dramatists of the time, served his playwright's apprenticeship under Henslowe, acquiring a journalistic competence and adaptability. Dekker was his master in the racy citizen comedies written for the children's companies; later, for the King's Men, he wrote the tragicomedies that Fletcher made popular in the second decade of the century. Success of a sort came with civic recognition. In 1620 he was appointed Chronologer to the City of London, responsible for writing and, apparently, directing official entertainments. The work demanded skill in rhetoric and in the handling of spectacle, talents which Middleton had demonstrated in masques and pageants for some years. His finest plays, *The Changeling* and *Women Beware Women*, belong to this period of public office. Assured of a steady income, perhaps Middleton felt free to write as he liked. He achieved fame with *A Game at Chess* (1624) in which English-Spanish politics were enacted on a chessboard—to the anger of the Spanish, the embarrassment of officialdom, and the great delight of English audiences, who packed the Globe for nine days before the play was suppressed.

The civic authorities began to show dissatisfaction with Middleton's pageant work, complaining of 'abuses and badd workmanship

---

[1] *The Works of Thomas Middleton*, ed. A. H. Bullen (1885–6), viii, 103–4.

in and about the contrivings and payntings' of the wagons; but he managed to retain his official post until his death in 1627.[2]

DATE

> I that have seen't can say, having just cause,
> Never came tragedy off with more applause.

When and where Nathaniel Richards saw *Women Beware Women* there is no knowing, for these lines of his, prefixed to the 1657 octavo of the play, are the only testimony that it was ever acted. Nor is there any record of an edition until 1653 when Moseley made his advance entry in the *Stationers' Register*. Middleton's contemporaries do not speak of the play, and its date must be determined from internal evidence alone. Two dates have been suggested—an early one (1613–14) and a later (*c.* 1621). J. I. Cope's argument for the former is based on a few similarities between the tragedy and the masque *Triumphs of Truth*, performed in October 1613.[3] But Middleton was always a repetitive writer; phrases and thoughts echo from one work to another and consequently tell us nothing about dating. Baldwin Maxwell, seeking to establish the later date, claims that the reference to stocking a new found land would have been topical in 1621 when the Virginia Company tried to launch its new colonising plan.[4] This is true; but the evidence loses its value when the idea is seen to be a repetition of a similar thought in *The Roaring Girl*, published in 1611 (see I, ii, 61 and *note*). Maxwell also makes the more valid point that Middleton is historically accurate about Bianca's age ('about sixteen', III, i, 180) but adds several years to the duke's to make him fifty-five—the age that James would have been in the summer of 1621; the king, Maxwell asserts, would have taken Bianca's compliment personally (see I, iii, 92–4).

In 1622 Sir Henry Herbert became Master of the Revels, and kept careful note of the plays he licensed. *Women Beware Women* is not one of them. It may have been 'allowed' before Herbert took office; alternatively, it may have been licensed under another title, not yet identified. Or perhaps Herbert's records are not fully comprehensive. Whether or not 1622 is accepted as the *terminus ad quem*, the later date is certainly to be preferred. The intricate weaving of plot with subplot, the boldly confident verse with its subtle ironies, and

---

[2] For a fuller account of Middleton's life see R. H. Barker, *Thomas Middleton* (1958).
[3] 'The Date of Middleton's *Women Beware Women*', *Modern Language Notes* 76 (1961).
[4] 'The Date of Middleton's *Women Beware Women*', *Philological Quarterly* XXII (1943).

the skilled selection of detail from the sources are the work of an experienced dramatist and a mature mind.

SOURCES

In the sixteenth century a Venetian heiress, Bianca Capello, fell in love with a bank-clerk and eloped with him to Florence. There the grand-duke saw her, loved her and, through the good offices of his friend Mondragone and Mondragone's wife, offered her the protection she needed. The duke and Bianca became lovers, while the complaisant husband, Pietro Buonaventura, boasted himself the lover of Cassandra, a rich Florentine widow. Cassandra's family, their pride outraged, complained to the duke, but Pietro ignored all kindly warnings of danger and was finally murdered as his two predecessors in Cassandra's love had been. Bianca grieved over his death until she was consoled by the duke.

This, in brief, is the story as it is told by Malespini in novels 84 and 85 of his *Ducento Novelle* (Venice, 1609). A conclusion is supplied by Fynes Moryson, who tells how the duke and Bianca married and were visited by the duke's cardinal brother:

> the Duchesse sent the Cardinall March payne for his breakfast, which he retorned with due Ceremony, saying that he did eate nothing but that was dressed by his owne Cooke, but the Duke by ill happ meeting the messenger, did eate a peece thereof, and when the Duchesse sawe it broken, shee smiled and spake some wordes of Joy, but the messenger telling her the Cardinalls Answer, and that the Duke had eaten that peece, shee with an unchanged Countenance tooke another peece, and having eaten it, locked herself in a clossett, and hereupon the Duke and shee dyed in one hower.
>
> (Moryson 4, 95)

The final part of Moryson's *Itinerary* was not published until 1903, but it is unnecessary to postulate that Middleton saw the MS. Italy, to the English mind, was a land of romance, intrigue and poison. Stories from Italy, especially if they could claim some foundation in fact, were repeated, multiplied and embroidered to satisfy an unceasing demand. Middleton almost certainly read Malespini, and probably filled in the gaps the novelist left by reading travellers' tales, letters, even official records.

In 1628 a pathetic little story was published, *The True History of the Tragicke Loves of Hipolito and Isabella Neapolitans*. This was an English version of an earlier (*c.* 1597) French fiction. Occasional verbal resemblances between parts of Middleton's play and this story suggest either that Middleton read the unpublished MS of the translation, or that the anonymous translator was somehow acquainted with the subplot of the play which must, in turn, be based on the French original. The two source-narratives merge in the character of Livia. Combining the rôles of the Italian Signora Mondragone and Cassandra, she also takes the part of the nun, Fabritio's sister, and the name of Fabritio's second wife. The same trick is used in play and novel to delude Isabella of her parentage so that she will consent to love her uncle under cover of marriage to a fool. But the father's mercenary desires and the details of the husband's brutal foolishness are of Middleton's invention.

THE PLAY

By most conventions of the drama Leantio's mother ought to be the embodiment of simple piety and honest good sense. This is the character she appears in at the start of the play, in her warm maternal welcome to her son; in the dignified apology to Bianca; and in her politely righteous answers to Livia's jesting. Yet even she has her price: 'here's an old wench would trot into a bawd now For some dry sucket or a colt in marchpane' (III, i, 269–70). Dazzled by affluence, she becomes the least victim of the materialist society of *Women Beware Women*. The immediate location of Middleton's play is Italy. The procession to St Mark's church, the Florentine bay-windows overlooking the street, the ladies' masks, the ceremony of betrothal—these give the local colour that the action demands. In other respects sixteenth-century Florence is seventeenth-century England, where a subsistence economy had given place too rapidly to an affluent society and where moralists, on or off the stage, were increasingly preoccupied with the problems of wealth and the use of riches. The comedies of Middleton and Dekker concentrate on the new possessors of these riches, the lower middle classes, and the moral is simple: in the loss of their traditional virtues of thrift and industry, the citizens have lost also that respect which is their due; and they have become ridiculous. Few writers, however, would venture a tragedy on such a theme, seeing that the pursuit of money diminished the character and denied the usual tragic stature. *Women Beware Women* is the greater achievement for being isolated. There is not a single character in the play who does not recognise the lure of gold. Even the duke, who can afford to ignore riches for himself, is alive to their persuasiveness when he bribes Bianca: 'Come, play the wise wench, and provide for ever' (II, ii, 383). The society he leads and represents identifies goodness with utility and measures status by possessions. When Bianca and Leantio find that they 'thrive best asunder' (IV, i, 61), they define their prosperity in terms of the new cloak, the spurs, the velvet chair—and, no doubt, the casting-bottle and green silk quilt whose lack the newly-seduced Bianca deplored. When material objects become so important, people become objects too—articles for use in trading. To Guardiano, although he repeats and endorses the duke's praise of her, Bianca is not a person but an instrument for his own advancement; her seduction by the duke would be 'much worth in wealth and favour' (II, ii, 23) to anyone who could engineer it. All sense of the human and individual is lost; and one would expect the sense of tragedy to be lost too. Yet Middleton's characters, even more than Webster's, are 'wretched, eminent things'.[5] As the duke's mistress Bianca is greedy for possessions and status, but she still retains something of her first gentleness. She dies with a kiss, although the heroic gesture is quickly lost when she looks round in panic: 'these are all strangers to me' (V, ii, 204). Affluence is wasteful, and the deeper human emotions are the most readily expendable. Married to the foolish Ward, Isabella will know only the misery of frustration; but this is of no consequence to her father. Survival is impossible without equivocation, so she must marry the Ward to satisfy the demands of society and sleep with Hippolito to find the love she needs herself. Similarly, but still more dangerously, the duke thinks to save his soul by marrying his whore after he has killed her husband. Their blindness makes these characters tragic. Like the 'blind folks' described by Leantio (IV, i, 95–6) they run up against the hard reality they cannot see, and the result is fatal.

The play's two plots combine to expose the cruelties of an acquisitive society. In the projected marriage of the Ward and Isabella, fantastically improvident though it now appears, Middleton was dramatising a common abuse, familiar enough to be commented on by a hack moralist:

> O how foolish is that father, that will bestow his well nourtured daughter in marriage with such a sot, that hath nothing in him but a joynture: these parents do little consider what a grievous fault they commit, in bringing their children to a loathed bed; and yet these faults amongest parents are too common.[6]

Without Livia's interference, and despite Isabella's professed intention to 'keep her days true to her husband, And know no other man' (I, ii, 163–4), such a marriage carries its own destruction. The casual assumption of the spectators, for whom Bianca and the duke are mouthpieces, is that Isabella will make other provision for her happiness: 'she'll find leisure To make that good enough' (III, ii, 210–11). There is, by contrast, true romance in the initial situation of Leantio and Bianca, young lovers who have defied parental wrath and

---

[5] *The Duchess of Malfi* V, v, 113.
[6] 'Barnaby Rich, *Faultes, Faults, and nothing else but Faultes* (1606), p. 26ᵛ.

considerations of dowry to elope together and to find content in each other and their love. But the pressures of society, operating on the two individuals as well as on their relationship, are overwhelming. The marriage-pattern of any society is decided by whichever sex is dominant in that society. Most usually (in Western civilisations) it is the male, and consequently the woman derives her status from her husband. Cinderella can then marry Prince Charming, and King Cophetua can wed the beggar-maid. These are extremes, but permissible extremes. Their opposite, involving what sociologists have labelled 'male hypergamy',[7] is not socially permissible: a man will not have the approval of society if he marries a woman who is his social superior. Recent fiction—such as *Room at the Top* and *Look Back in Anger*—has done much to bring this to our consciousness, but the dilemma is not of twentieth-century origin. Bianca is always aware of what she has sacrificed for Leantio's love, and the duke's reminder is one of the most potent arguments in her seduction:

> Do not I know y'have cast away your life
> Upon necessities, means merely doubtful
> To keep you in indifferent health and fashion.
>
> II, ii, 376–8

Love is no more adequate than money as the basis for marriage: this is the grim conclusion of Middleton's play. Plot and subplot are interwoven, the one counterpointing the other. Yet critics have spoken of the 'tedious, almost irrelevant' clowning,[8] the 'silly and only fortuitously connected comic subplots'[9] which mar both *The Changeling* and *Women Beware Women*. It was Middleton's intention that the Ward should be tedious. So far as he is concerned, Isabella is only a legitimate and more expensive version of the larder-woman and the kitchen-wench: a body that will serve the turn of his much-boasted virility. At first sight he is comic enough, but with each subsequent appearance the humour diminishes as the obscenity grows. Yet the more crudely he shows himself, the less is Isabella affected. She suffers his impertinent questions, even his snooping under her skirts, with a cold disdain that is far removed from the anguish of her first encounter with him. Duplicity has coarsened her. In the same way Bianca exchanges girlish innocence for worldly-wise sophistication, and her creamy acceptance of lodgings provided by the duke—'Your love is great, my lord' (III, ii, 241)—contrasts forcefully with her welcome to Leantio's poor home:

[7] See Geoffrey Gorer, 'The Perils of Hypergamy', *New Statesman* 53, 4 May 1957.
[8] Samuel Schoenbaum, *Middleton's Tragedies* (New York, 1955), p. 103.
[9] Madeleine Doran, *Endeavors of Art* (Madison, 1954), p. 179.

Kind mother, there is nothing can be wanting
To her that does enjoy all her desires.

I, i, 125–6

In such contrasts, implied more often than spoken, is the heart of the play; its real value lies not in the cynical conclusion, but in the demonstration of character responding to circumstance and being changed by it.

Emotionally and morally, these characters are cripples. Fabritio and the Ward are near kin in their deformities, and the Ward is only a gross parody of his father-in-law. The source's Fabritio was

a Gentleman . . . who as well for the much desert of his vertues, as for the nobleness of his descent, held the place of one of the most honoured Magistrates of the Citie.

Hipolito & Isabella, p. 3

In the play he is a trader: his daughter is an investment and marriage a stock-exchange. Isabella is a 'dear child' (III, ii, 107 *ff.*)—dear, as her father says, to his purse—and her education has had a single end in view:

I have brought her up to music, dancing, what not,
That may commend her sex and stir her husband.

III, ii, 112–3

To the Ward marriage is a cattle-market, and Isabella an animal to be 'bought and sold and turned and pried into' (III, iii, 35). At the banquet she is led out to show her paces in the dance; later her teeth are inspected. These two, Fabritio and the Ward, are static characters —the same fools at the end as they are at the beginning; but their foolishness is no longer funny. There is more development in Hippolito, who is not at all the 'rather conventional figure' seen by Barker, 'colorless early in the play and inconsistent later'.[10] The initial perplexity, as he regards a passion which he knows to be wrong but which he makes no obvious efforts to overcome, resolves itself by maintaining a dual standard of conduct and morality. Vice must be hidden; there is 'a blind time made' for sin (IV, ii, 5), and because Leantio's openness will not observe the rules, he must die. Hippolito, outwardly respectable but inwardly corrupt, shares his double standard with Guardiano, the 'kind, honest, courteous gentleman' (II, ii, 453) with his 'smooth-browed treachery' (II, ii, 429). Both recognise a specious 'honour' which must be served but which is totally unconnected with their private lives; and both, as the duke perceptively observes of Hippolito, have a sensitivity that arises from guilt:

[10] *Op. cit.*, p. 138.

The ulcerous reputation feels the poise
Of lightest wrongs, as sores are vexed with flies.

IV, i, 138–9

Leantio too is aware of guilt, but in his case the effect is paralysing. He is obsessed with his crime in stealing Bianca from her home even when he boasts of his success. A pathetic figure, he is the victim of a social disease for which he is not responsible, a type of the 'small house agent's clerk' in *The Waste Land*:

One of the low on whom assurance sits
As a silk hat on a Bradford millionaire.

A weekend love is all that his station in life can afford; he owns a jewel now, but can only enjoy it after working-hours. He has been abused for his 'coarseness of mind',[11] and for a 'point of view [which] is hopelessly bourgeois'.[12] Leantio, certainly, is not the dashing hero of romantic fiction. A pious, penny-pinching virtue marks even his proudest moments, and however gallantly he tries to appear affectionate, he succeeds only in embarrassing. Yet when he speaks of Bianca as his 'treasure', his 'life's wealth', it is not a perversion that is revealed but rather a deficiency. Leantio cannot think in any other way. Proverbs, or phrases with a proverbial ring, abound in his speeches; he talks and feels in cliché. After his one decisive action, the 'theft' of Bianca, Leantio can do nothing but accept. The captainship of the fort, the fine clothes, and at last his death are all received passively, with a mixture of surprise and resentment. Hippolito has an unfair advantage in the duel, and Leantio dies in sad confusion. This was made very clear in a 1962 production of the play, reviewed by Kenneth Tynan:

You know from the panicky way in which he fumbles and flinches that this is the first time he has ever wielded the expensive sword that hangs at his waist; he grips the hilt with both hands, and looks stupid as he is spitted, dying not comically or tragically, but in a state of bewildered unbelief.[13]

Leantio is Middleton's own creation. Bianca's husband in Malespini's *novelle* is an easy-going cuckold, content for the most part to accept the duke's favours to his wife, since they increase his security and permit a liaison with the rich widow. Only in their verbal fencing match (IV, i) do the play's Bianca and Leantio bear a close resemblance to the source's Bianca and Pietro, and even here the motivation of the dramatic characters comes from within and not

---

[11] Christopher Ricks, 'Word Play in *Women Beware Women*', *Review of English Studies* NS 12 (1961), p. 249.
[12] Schoenbaum, *op. cit.*, p. 111.
[13] *The Observer*, 8 July 1962.

from the inspiration of the source. Middleton again abandons Malespini for the character of the duke; but whereas he created a new individual in Leantio, he achieves this time only the conventional royal lecher of Italianate tragedy, a shadowy figure who draws what strength he possesses from the society Middleton places him in.

Especially for the duke, but generally for all his male characters, Middleton had a strong dramatic tradition to influence him and to offer suggestions, however slight. Of the female characters, however, only the Mother owes much to convention; she quickly serves her purpose and is dropped from the action. Middleton is rightly praised for his understanding of female psychology:

> Middleton's capacity for tragedy is inseparable from his other supreme gift, his discernment of the minds of women; in this no dramatist of the period except Shakespeare is his equal, at once for variety and penetration.[14]

The comparison with Shakespeare is no more than just, and without denying the achievement in Lady Macbeth, Cleopatra and Isabella it must be claimed for Middleton that he enters an area of female experience untouched by Shakespeare. Through Bianca and Isabella in *Women Beware Women*, and through Beatrice-Joanna in *The Changeling*, he charts the slow awakening to sin and reality as gentle, impetuous girls change into ruthless, scheming women.

There is always the danger that hindsight may be blinding—that a character may be wrongly assessed in his opening scenes by an assumption that he is the same then that he is at the end. Thus Schoenbaum describes a 'wholly sensual' relationship between Leantio and Bianca from the first,[15] and Eliot regards Bianca as 'a woman of the type who is purely moved by vanity'.[16] Eliot's is the criticism more seriously at fault; it leaves no room for the play to do its work in. Bianca's meek silence, followed by the statement of content with cottage poverty, must be taken at face value, along with her protestations of virtue to the duke. Only in this way can her subsequent cruelty have its full impact. Seduction makes Bianca articulate; and her eloquence is feminine, especially in the frequent pointed recall of the past and her hurtful reminders of the elopement:

> Nay, were't yourself, whose love had power, you know,
> To bring me from my friends, I would not stand thus
> And gaze upon you always.

> III, i, 140–2

---

[14] Una Ellis-Fermor, *The Jacobean Drama* (1936, 2nd ed. 1947), p. 149.
[15] *Op. cit.*, p. 117.
[16] 'Thomas Middleton', *Selected Essays* (3rd ed. 1951), p. 166.

Adroitly, she turns Leantio's arguments against him:

> 'Tis time to leave off dalliance; 'tis a doctrine
> Of your own teaching, if you be remembered,
> And I was bound to obey it.
>
> III, i, 168–70

In the scene of inventoried jealousy between the duke's mistress and Livia's lover it is Bianca who comes off best. Leantio loses his temper, but Bianca does not falter until it is all over. Her control is marked by the repeated 'sir', an elegant afterthought lingering to taunt Leantio at the end of every line:

LEANTIO
  A chair of velvet!
BIANCA   Is your cloak lined through, sir?
LEANTIO
  Y'are very stately here.
BIANCA   'Faith, something proud, sir.

IV, i, 53–4

After this 'glistering whore' display it is not easy to contrive a tragic death for Bianca, but Middleton can now use his subplot, with its dramatic eruptions and revelations, to draw the attention away from Bianca for the next scene or two, giving her only a brief moment of reformed piety when she reproaches the cardinal for his want of charity. With less than total success, Middleton then tries at the end to recapitulate the complexity of Bianca's life—her love for the duke, a sense of sin, her guilt towards Leantio, and a final dying morality. All but the first of these might well have been forgotten. Of her dying utterances the best, because the most realistic and psychologically consistent, comes with the frightened glance round the hostile court:

> What make I here? these are all strangers to me,
> Not known but by their malice, now th'art gone.
>
> V, ii, 204–5

In the game of chess Bianca is a pawn, and like a pawn's her movements are restricted; she can never turn back: 'Your pawn cannot come back to relieve itself' (II, ii, 303). She is matched against the queen, Livia, a far more powerful piece that can twist and turn in any direction. Middleton's chess allusions are no more than random, appropriate only as isolated moves and not as a complete game throughout the play, but even so they are made to serve a dual purpose. Livia's comments on her match with the Mother describe the action taking place offstage between Bianca and the duke, the 'black king [who] makes all the haste he can' (II, ii, 391); and the game also helps to define the character of Livia:

It endorses in highly dramatic terms the way in which Livia consistently uses other people as pawns in what is to her a fascinating game.[17]

The direct link between plot and subplot, combining the roles of Signora Mondragone, Cassandra and the nun from the two sources, Livia is the greatest of Middleton's character creations. In her wit and vitality she is a Chaucerian figure, and the critical humour with which she is presented has also its precedent in Chaucer. Lamb, quoting the dialogue before Livia and the Mother settle down to their game, remarked

> This is one of those scenes which has the air of being an immediate transcript from life. Livia the 'good neighbour' is as real a creature as one of Chaucer's characters. She is such another jolly Housewife as the Wife of Bath.[18]

Compared with Livia, however, the Wife of Bath is a simple character; the details Chaucer gives radiate with a centrifugal force from a single idea. Middleton's technique is the opposite. Livia constantly surprises, and as each new facet is revealed it modifies the rest. At first she sets up a humane opposition to her brother's heartless matchmaking, but the response to this cannot be wholly approving; while recognising love and the need for love, Livia also extends an amused tolerance to casual lapses:

> And if we lick a finger then, sometimes,
> We are not too blame; your best cooks use it.
>
> I, ii, 44-5

Irving Ribner, who stresses the importance of the reiterated food images in the play, notes that with these lines

> We are made at once aware that she lives in the same moral climate as her brother and that her values are no different from his.[19]

More depth is given to the character when she encounters Hippolito: 'thou art all a feast' (I, ii, 151). Her tenderness towards him and her readiness to serve his will at whatever cost to herself and her own 'honesty' speak a more than natural affection and hint a one-sided incestuous attraction.[20] If this is admitted, then the procuring of Isabella seems less like an evil game and more an attempt to provide

---

[17] G. R. Hibbard, 'The Tragedies of Thomas Middleton and the Decadence of the Drama', *Renaissance and Modern Studies* 1 (1957), p. 50.
[18] *Specimens of the English Dramatic Poets* (1808), p. 155.
[19] 'Middleton's *Women Beware Women*', *Tulane Studies in English* IX (1959), p. 31.
[20] A point which is suggested in the source (see note at II, i, 26–7), and which is fully discussed by Daniel Dodson in 'Middleton's Livia', *Philological Quarterly* XXVII (1948).

some acceptable substitute for herself. Through Isabella Livia can indulge, vicariously, her own desires. By the end of the second Act a formidable and complex personality has imposed itself on the other characters. Self-possessed and in command of all the situations she has created, Livia seems invulnerable. And then, with the banquet scene, Middleton begins to strip away the façade. Livia's cunning is forgotten in the rush of passion, and she almost deludes herself into thinking that Leantio might return the feeling:

> I am not yet so old, but he may think of me.
> My own fault—I have been idle a long time;
> But I'll begin the week and paint tomorrow.
>
> III, ii, 141–3

The clumsiness of the approach becomes apparent even to Livia herself, and as the scene ends she has regained some of her diplomacy and accepted the fact that she will have to buy her lover. The same pattern is repeated at Leantio's death, when a surge of emotion again breaks through the poise and has to be suppressed into scheming. Livia's last words—'My own ambition pulls me down to ruin' (V, ii, 131)—are meaningless. They give her a line to die on and nothing more. But the character who started, it seems, as an organisational device, finishes by dominating the play.

Unlike most tragedies, where the interest is compelled by two or three foreground figures while the rest of the *dramatis personae* function out of the limelight, *Women Beware Women* has only two characters—Sordido and the Cardinal—who do not call for a complex response. We react, however, intellectually and not emotionally; the play is cruel but oddly unmoving. One cause of this reaction is the unusually large number of complicated characters; another, closely related to the first, is the speed of the play. There is no time for deep emotional involvement. In the climactic banquet scene, for instance, the technique is that of the film camera which focuses on each character in turn, catches a word or a look, then passes to the next. As soon as one impression has been registered, another is superimposed. Just as quickly, one episode succeeds another as the action cuts between plot and subplot. The verse too has a swift economy, most remarkable in the frequent asides spoken, as it were, in the short breathing-space between the end of one line and the beginning of the next; and in the many single lines divided between speakers, where one character's thought is taken up or interrupted by another. Middleton's is a plain style where images, though plentiful, are rarely extended. Food imagery is used as systematically throughout this play as it is in *Troilus and Cressida*, but it is less conspicuous. Leantio compares marriage to a 'banqueting-house' (III, i, 90); Livia declares that her brother is 'all a feast' (I, ii, 151);

and Isabella reconciles herself to 'some choice cates then once a week' (II, i, 223) in Hippolito's love. By such reiterated images Middleton 'links the moral position of his various characters',[21] suggesting all the time a greediness and a self-indulgence in their feelings. Used just as consistently, the language of trade and finance carries, often in a single word, both a meaning and an attitude to that meaning; both must be apprehended simultaneously and at speed. This, and the understanding of the many *doubles entendres*, is an intellectual activity, demanding the detachment of wit and not the involvement of feeling. There is, however, a marked slowing down with the entry of the Cardinal. Speeches lengthen and images are extended as Middleton makes a misguided grab for the emotions. The Cardinal utters a string of truisms, Elizabethan commonplaces on the responsibilities of a ruler and the uncertainty of human life, which have the strength of tradition but no originality. An external moral judgement is imported, and flabbiness threatens: 'Until he [the Cardinal] appears the play does its own work'.[22]

The last scene makes up for the jog-trot moralising. Ever since Kyd introduced the slaughterous playlet at the end of *The Spanish Tragedy* dramatists took careful note of the advice formulated by the author of *The Revenger's Tragedy*:

> A mask is treason's licence: that build upon—
> 'Tis murder's best face, when a vizard's on.
>
> V, i, 176–7

The play gallops to an unashamedly theatrical conclusion. A strict poetic justice is handed out—to Livia, suffocated with the incense offered to the marriage-goddess; to Hippolito, shot with cupids' arrows; to Guardiano, spiked on his own caltrop. The ingenuity which makes every punishment fit its crime is proof enough that this ending was not the conventional last resort of a tired dramatist whose inspiration had run dry. Similar racing endings to Middleton's early comedies have been explained by Una Ellis-Fermor as

> due not so much to carelessness on the part of the author as to an understanding of the psychological condition of an audience at the end of a comedy intrigue. Once they have foreseen the end they only want it sketched, not expounded.[23]

To a twentieth-century mind the masque with its murders is disconcerting and the wit seems to be misplaced; yet this can be overcome by remembering the poisoned pictures, skulls and helmets of other revenge tragedies and the delight of murderers, dramatists and audiences alike in the deft handling of an Italianate revenge:

---

[21] Ribner, *op. cit.*, p. 28.
[22] Hibbard, *op. cit.*, p. 53.   [23] *Op. cit.*, p. 133 *note*.

I would have our plot be ingenious,
And have it hereafter recorded for example
Rather than borrow example.

                              (*The White Devil*, V, i, 74–6)

Middleton passes this final test of his stagecraft, the competition for ingenuity, with honours; and by their deaths the characters are redeemed. Deprived of the convention of the masque, Middleton would have had to leave them alive, without salvation in an infinity of soulless intrigue.

NOTE ON THE TEXT

THE EARLIEST edition of *Women Beware Women* is the octavo printed for Humphrey Moseley in 1657, and one of the nineteen surviving copies of this (Bodleian 8° C 19 ART BS) has been taken as the foundation of the present text. Moseley took great pains to print accurately, and collation of several copies of O shows minute press correction, hardly ever of a substantial nature. The MS used in printing may have been Middleton's own papers, annotated by a theatrical book-keeper: the stage directions show both the precision needed for a stage presentation (as at II, ii, 177) and the vagueness (as at I, iii, 72) that is more characteristic of an author. For this edition spelling has been modernised and the punctuation lightened. The many asides have not been marked as such, since their nature is usually self-evident; but where there is a sudden change of thought-direction this has been indicated by an introductory dash. An attempt has been made to disentangle O's occasional jumbling of verse and prose.

Two of Middleton's stylistic idiosyncrasies need to be noted. The speed of his writing is encouraged by numerous elisions—such as *o'th'* for *of the* and *i'th'* for *in the*—to which he can give monosyllabic weighting. His fondness for *nev'r, ev'r* and *ev'n* is part of this trait. To expand to *never, ever* and *even* adds an extra syllable, while adoption of the conventional *ne'er, e'er* and *e'en* detracts, by the omission of the hard consonant, from the masculine crispness of the sound. I have therefore retained O's forms in this matter. I have also followed O in printing *too blame* where *to blame* would seem the obvious modernisation. In the sixteenth and seventeenth centuries the dative infinitive was often misunderstood: *blame* was taken to be an adjective and *to* as the adverb *too*. This is clearly seen in *1 Henry IV's* 'In faith, my lord, you are too wilful blame' (III, i, 177).

Notes to the play are divided into the textual and simple explanatory (printed above the rule at the foot of the relevant page); and the more detailed or critical (printed below the rule). The *double entendre* is frequent in this play. Rather than offer a ponderous explanation of a delicate obscenity I have tried to adduce passages from Middleton's own work, or from his contemporaries', where the intention is the same but less obscure.

FURTHER READING

Bradbrook, M. C. *Themes and Conventions of Elizabethan Tragedy* (1935), ch. ix.

Dodson, Daniel. 'Middleton's Livia', *Philological Quarterly* (1948).

Ellis-Fermor, Una. *The Jacobean Drama* (2nd ed. 1947), ch. VII.

Hibbard, G. R. 'The Tragedies of Thomas Middleton', *Renaissance and Modern Studies* vol. 1 (1957).

Ribner, Irving. 'Middleton's *Women Beware Women*', *Tulane Studies in English* IX (1959).

Ricks, Christopher. 'Word Play in *Women Beware Women*', *Review of English Studies* NS12 (1961).

WOMEN
BEWARE
WOMEN.

A
TRAGEDY,
BY
Tho. Middleton, Gent.

LONDON:
Printed for *Humphrey Moseley*, 1657.

TO THE READER

<small>WHEN THESE</small>[1] amongst others of Mr Thomas Middleton's excellent poems came to my hands, I was not a little confident but that his name would prove as great an inducement for thee to read, as me to print them, since those issues of his brain that have already seen the sun have by their worth gained themselves a free entertainment amongst all that are ingenious; and I am most certain that these will no way lessen his reputation, nor hinder his admission to any noble and recreative spirits. All that I require at thy hands, is to continue the author in his deserved esteem, and to accept of my endeavours which have ever been to please thee.

Farewell

Upon the Tragedy of My Familiar Acquaintance Tho. Middleton

> *Women beware Women:* 'tis a true text
> Never to be forgot. Drabs of state vexed
> Have plots, poisons, mischiefs that seldom miss
> To murther virtue with a venom kiss—
> Witness this worthy tragedy, expressed
> By him that well deserved amongst the best
> Of poets in his time. He knew the rage,
> Madness of women crossed; and for the stage
> Fitted their humours, hell-bred malice, strife
> Acted in state, presented to the life.
> I that have seen't can say, having just cause,
> Never came tragedy off with more applause.

Nath. Richards[2]

---

[1] *Women Beware Women* was printed along with *More Dissemblers Besides Women.*
[2] Nathaniel Richards (*fl* 1630–54) was author of *The Tragedy of Messallina.*

[DRAMATIS PERSONAE]

DUKE OF FLORENCE
LORD CARDINAL, *brother to the* DUKE
TWO CARDINALS *more*
A LORD
FABRITIO, *father to* ISABELLA
HIPPOLITO, *brother to* FABRITIO
GUARDIANO, *uncle to the foolish* WARD
THE WARD, *a rich young heir*
LEANTIO, *a factor, husband to* BIANCA
SORDIDO, *the* WARD'S *man*

LIVIA, *sister to* FABRITIO
ISABELLA, *niece to* LIVIA
BIANCA, LEANTIO'S *wife*
THE WIDOW, *his* [LEANTIO'S] *mother*
STATES OF FLORENCE, CITIZENS, A 'PRENTICE, BOYS, MESSENGER,
    SERVANTS
[TWO LADIES, *other* LORDS, PAGES, GUARD]

The Scene:
FLORENCE.

9 *factor* agent
15 *States* Nobility

---

13 BIANCA. O's *Brancha* (here and throughout the play) probably
represents a misreading of MS's *i* as *r*.

5

WOMEN BEWARE WOMEN

Act I, Scene i

Enter LEANTIO *with* BIANCA *and* MOTHER

MOTHER
    Thy sight was never yet more precious to me;
    Welcome, with all the affection of a mother,
    That comfort can express from natural love:
    Since thy birth-joy—a mother's chiefest gladness
    After sh'as undergone her curse of sorrows—   5
    Thou wast not more dear to me, than this hour
    Presents thee to my heart. Welcome again.

LEANTIO
    'Las, poor affectionate soul, how her joys speak to me!
    I have observed it often, and I know it is
    The fortune commonly of knavish children   10
    To have the loving'st mothers.

MOTHER   What's this gentlewoman?

LEANTIO
    Oh you have named the most unvalued'st purchase,
    That youth of man had ever knowledge of.
    As often as I look upon that treasure,
    And know it to be mine—there lies the blessing—   15
    It joys me that I ever was ordained
    To have a being, and to live 'mongst men;
    Which is a fearful living, and a poor one,
    Let a man truly think on't,
    To have the toil and griefs of fourscore years   20
    Put up in a white sheet, tied with two knots.
    Methinks it should strike earthquakes in adulterers,
    When ev'n the very sheets they commit sin in,
    May prove, for aught they know, all their last garments.
    Oh what a mark were there for women then!   25
    But beauty able to content a conqueror,

3 *express* distil
12 *unvalued'st* invaluable   12 *purchase* theft

---

21 *two knots.* The deathbed portrait of Donne shows how the shroud was
    fastened with a knot at head and feet.
26–7 *conqueror . . . content.* Alexander the Great is said to have wept because
    there were no new worlds for him to conquer.

Whom earth could scarce content, keeps me in compass;
I find no wish in me bent sinfully
To this man's sister, or to that man's wife:
In love's name let 'em keep their honesties,   30
And cleave to their own husbands, 'tis their duties.
Now when I go to church, I can pray handsomely;
Nor come like gallants only to see faces,
As if lust went to market still on Sundays.
I must confess I am guilty of one sin, mother,   35
More than I brought into the world with me;
But that I glory in: 'tis theft, but noble
As ever greatness yet shot up withal.

MOTHER
How's that?

LEANTIO   Never to be repented, mother,
Though sin be death! I had died, if I had not sinned,   40
And here's my masterpiece. Do you now behold her!
Look on her well, she's mine; look on her better—
Now say, if't be not the best piece of theft
That ever was committed. And I have my pardon for't:
'Tis sealed from Heaven by marriage.

MOTHER   Married to her!   45

LEANTIO
You must keep council mother, I am undone else;
If it be known, I have lost her. Do but think now
What that loss is—life's but a trifle to't.
From Venice her consent and I have brought her,
From parents great in wealth, more now in rage;   50
But let storms spend their furies. Now we have got
A shelter o'er our quiet innocent loves,
We are contented. Little money sh'as brought me:
View but her face, you may see all her dowry,
Save that which lies locked up in hidden virtues,   55
Like jewels kept in cabinets.

MOTHER   Y'are too blame,
If your obedience will give way to a check,
To wrong such a perfection.

LEANTIO   How?

27 *in compass* within limits
56 *too blame* See Note on the Text, p. xxvii

32–4 *Now . . . Sundays.* '. . . come abroad where matter is frequent, to
court, to tiltings, publique showes, and feasts, and church sometimes . . .
In these places a man shall find whom to love, whom to play with,
whom to touch once, whom to hold ever' (Jonson, *Epicoene*, IV, i, 57–62).

MOTHER   Such a creature,
  To draw her from her fortune, which no doubt,
  At the full time, might have proved rich and noble: 60
  You know not what you have done. My life can give you
  But little helps, and my death lesser hopes;
  And hitherto your own means has but made shift
  To keep you single, and that hardly too.
  What ableness have you to do her right, then,   65
  In maintenance fitting her birth and virtues,
  Which ev'ry woman of necessity looks for,
  And most to go above it, not confined
  By their conditions, virtues, bloods, or births,
  But flowing to affections, wills and humours?   70
LEANTIO
  Speak low sweet mother; you are able to spoil as many
  As come within the hearing; if it be not
  Your fortune to mar all, I have much marvel.
  I pray do not you teach her to rebel,
  When she's in a good way to obedience;   75
  To rise with other women in commotion
  Against their husbands, for six gowns a year,
  And so maintain their cause, when they're once up,
  In all things else that require cost enough.
  They are all of 'em a kind of spirits—soon raised,   80
  But not so soon laid, mother. As for example,
  A woman's belly is got up in a trice:
  A simple charge ere it be laid down again:
  So ever in all their quarrels, and their courses.
  And I'm a proud man, I hear nothing of 'em;   85
  They're very still, I thank my happiness,
  And sound asleep; pray let not your tongue wake 'em.
  If you can but rest quiet, she's contented
  With all conditions that my fortunes bring her to:
  To keep close as a wife that loves her husband;   90
  To go after the rate of my ability,
  Not the licentious swindge of her own will,
  Like some of her old schoolfellows. She intends

84 *courses* actions

---

83 *A simple charge.* Either this must be spoken with a heavy irony (which
     to my mind is not appropriate here); or it must be allowed that Middle-
     ton is using *simple* in a sense not recorded by *O.E.D.* similar to his use
     of *simply* (= absolutely) at, for instance, IV, i, 43.
92 *swindge.* Sway: 'They give the full swindge to their bold and violent
     affections' (Beard, *Theatre of God's Judgements*, p. 272).

To take out other works in a new sampler,
And frame the fashion of an honest love,   95
Which knows no wants but, mocking poverty,
Brings forth more children, to make rich men wonder
At divine Providence, that feeds mouths of infants,
And sends them none to feed, but stuffs their rooms
With fruitful bags, their beds with barren wombs.   100
Good mother, make not you things worse than they are
Out of your too much openness—pray take heed on't—
Nor imitate the envy of old people,
That strive to mar good sport, because they are perfect.
I would have you more pitiful to youth,   105
Especially to your own flesh and blood.
I'll prove an excellent husband—here's my hand—
Lay in provision, follow my business roundly,
And make you a grandmother in forty weeks!
Go, pray salute her, bid her welcome cheerfully.   110

MOTHER
Gentlewoman, thus much is a debt of courtesy
                              [*she kisses* BIANCA]
Which fashionable strangers pay each other
At a kind meeting; then there's more than one,
Due to the knowledge I have of your nearness;
I am bold to come again, and now salute you   115
By th'name of daughter, which may challenge more
Than ordinary respect.

LEANTIO   Why, this is well now,
And I think few mothers of threescore will mend it.

MOTHER
What I can bid you welcome to, is mean;
But make it all your own: we are full of wants,   120
And cannot welcome worth.

LEANTIO   Now this is scurvy,
And spoke as if a woman lacked her teeth!
These old folks talk of nothing but defects,
Because they grow so full of 'em themselves.

BIANCA
Kind mother, there is nothing can be wanting   125
To her that does enjoy all her desires.

104 *perfect* contented (*O.E.D.* 7)
122 *spoke* ed (spake O)

---

100 *fruitful . . . wombs.* 'Where bags are fruitful'st there the womb's most
  barren' (Middleton, *Michaelmas Term*, Induction, line 25).
121–2 *scurvy . . . teeth.* One of the symptoms of scurvy is loss of teeth.

Heaven send a quiet peace with this man's love,
And I am as rich, as virtue can be poor—
Which were enough, after the rate of mind,
To erect temples for content placed here.   130
I have forsook friends, fortunes, and my country;
And hourly I rejoice in't. Here's my friends,
And few is the good number. Thy successes,
Howe'er they look, I will still name my fortunes;
Hopeful or spiteful, they shall all be welcome: 135
Who invites many guests, has of all sorts
As he that traffics much, drinks of all fortunes:
Yet they must all be welcome, and used well.
I'll call this place the place of my birth now—
And rightly too, for here my love was born,   140
And that's the birthday of a woman's joys.
You have not bid me welcome since I came.

LEANTIO
That I did, questionless.

BIANCA   No sure, how was't?
I have quite forgot it.

LEANTIO   Thus. [*kisses her*]

BIANCA   Oh sir, 'tis true,
Now I remember well: I have done thee wrong,   145
Pray take't again, sir. [*kisses him*]

LEANTIO   How many of these wrongs
Could I put up in an hour? and turn up the glass
For twice as many more.

MOTHER
Will't please you to walk in, daughter?

BIANCA   Thanks, sweet
                                              mother;
The voice of her that bare me is not more pleasing.   150
                    Exeunt [MOTHER *and* BIANCA]

LEANTIO
Though my own care and my rich master's trust
Lay their commands both on my factorship,
This day and night I'll know no other business
But her and her dear welcome. 'Tis a bitterness
To think upon tomorrow, that I must leave her   155
Still to the sweet hopes of the week's end.
That pleasure should be so restrained and curbed
After the course of a rich workmaster,
That never pays till Saturday night!

147 *turn up the glass* reverse the hour-glass

Marry, it comes together in a round sum then,   160
And does more good, you'll say. Oh fair-eyed Florence!
Didst thou but know what a most matchless jewel
Thou now art mistress of, a pride would take thee
Able to shoot destruction through the bloods
Of all thy youthful sons! But 'tis great policy   165
To keep choice treasures in obscurest places:
Should we show thieves our wealth, 'twould make 'em bolder.
Temptation is a devil will not stick
To fasten upon a saint—take heed of that.
The jewel is cased up from all men's eyes: 170
Who could imagine now a gem were kept,
Of that great value, under this plain roof?
But how in times of absence—what assurance
Of this restraint then? yes, yes—there's one with her!
Old mothers know the world; and such as these,   175
When sons lock chests, are good to look to keys.   *Exit*

Act I, Scene ii

Enter GUARDIANO, FABRITIO, *and* LIVIA [*with* SERVANT]

GUARDIANO
What, has your daughter seen him yet? know you that?
FABRITIO
No matter—she shall love him.
GUARDIANO   Nay, let's have fair play!
He has been now my ward some fifteen year,
And 'tis my purpose, as time calls upon me,
By custom seconded, and such moral virtues,   5
To tender him a wife; now, sir, this wife
I'ld fain elect out of a daughter of yours.
You see my meaning's fair. If now this daughter,
So tendered—let me come to your own phrase, sir—
Should offer to refuse him, I were handselled.   10
—Thus am I fain to calculate all my words
For the meridian of a foolish old man,
To take his understanding! What do you answer, sir?

12 *meridian* point of highest development

175–6 *Old mothers . . . keys.* '. . . the poor wife sits alone at home, **locked**
    upp and kept by old women' (Moryson 4, p. 151).
10 *handselled.* A *handsel*, literally, is a New Year's gift; the ironic use **of the**
    verb (as here) is not uncommon.

FABRITIO
  I say still, she shall love him.

GUARDIANO   Yet again?
  And shall she have no reason for this love?   15

FABRITIO
  Why, do you think that women love with reason?

GUARDIANO
  I perceive fools are not at all hours foolish,
  No more than wisemen wise.

FABRITIO   I had a wife;
  She ran mad for me; she had no reason for't
  For aught I could perceive. What think you,   20
  Lady sister?

GUARDIANO   —'Twas a fit match that,
  Being both out of their wits! A loving wife, 'seemed,
  She strove to come as near you as she could.

FABRITIO
  And if her daughter prove not mad for love too,
  She takes not after her—nor after me,   25
  If she prefer reason before my pleasure.
  You're an experienced widow, lady sister;
  I pray let your opinion come amongst us.

LIVIA
  I must offend you then, if truth will do't,
  And take my niece's part, and call't injustice   30
  To force her love to one she never saw.
  Maids should both see and like—all little enough:
  If they love truly after that, 'tis well.
  Counting the time, she takes one man till death,
  That's a hard task, I tell you; but one may   35
  Enquire at three years' end amongst young wives,
  And mark how the game goes.

FABRITIO   Why, is not man
  Tied to the same observance, lady sister,
  And in one woman?

LIVIA   'Tis enough for him;
  Besides, he tastes of many sundry dishes   40
  That we poor wretches never lay our lips to—
  As obedience, forsooth, subjection, duty, and such kickshaws,
  All of our making, but served in to them;

---

42 *kickshaws* fancy dishes

---

17 *fools . . . foolish.* Proverbial: 'Even a fool sometimes speaks a wise word'
  (Tilley, F 449).

And if we lick a finger then, sometimes,
We are not too blame; your best cooks use it.   45
FABRITIO
Th'art a sweet lady, sister, and a witty.
LIVIA
A witty! Oh, the bud of commendation,
Fit for a girl of sixteen! I am blown, man!
I should be wise by this time—and, for instance,
I have buried my two husbands in good fashion,   50
And never mean more to marry.
GUARDIANO   No, why so, lady?
LIVIA
Because the third shall never bury me:
I think I am more than witty. How think you, sir?
FABRITIO
I have paid often fees to a counsellor
Has had a weaker brain.
LIVIA   Then I must tell you,   55
Your money was soon parted.
GUARDIANO   Light her now, brother!
LIVIA
Where is my niece? let her be sent for straight.

                                        [*Exit* SERVANT]

---

45 *use* are in the habit of doing

---

45 *best cooks.* Proverbial: 'He is an ill cook that cannot lick his own fingers' (Tilley, C 636).

48 *blown.* Fully blossomed—but with a sense of being past the best: 'Against the blown rose may they stop their nose, That kneel'd unto the buds' (*Antony and Cleopatra*, III, xiii, 39-40). Simpson suggests that *blown woman* would be a more appropriate reading; but the jocular *man* is characteristic of Middleton's experienced women (cf. Livia again at II, i, 40, and *The Witch*, II, ii, 127: 'we're all flesh and blood, man').

56 *money . . . parted.* Proverbial: 'A fool and his money are soon parted' (Tilley, F 452).

56 *Light her now, brother.* O. Bullen, also following O, suggests the emendation *Like enow* (giving *brother* to Livia in the next line) and reminds that there is no great difference in pronunciation between *Light her now* and *Like enow*. This reasoning can only be valid, however, if we postulate some oral stage in the transmission of the text. Simpson (also giving *brother* to Livia) recommends that Guardiano should say *Plight her now*—i.e. 'settle the business on the spot'. But this reading attributes an urgency to the character which is at odds with his earlier wishes to wait some little time. In the absence of any convincing alternative I have adhered to O; perhaps Guardiano is inciting Fabritio to answer Livia, to bring her down, now she is in full, witty flight?

If you have any hope 'twill prove a wedding,
'Tis fit i'faith she should have one sight of him,
And stop upon't, and not be joined in haste,   60
As if they went to stock a new found land.

FABRITIO

Look out her uncle, and y'are sure of her,
Those two are nev'r asunder; they've been heard
In argument at midnight, moonshine nights
Are noondays with them; they walk out their sleeps—   65
Or rather at those hours appear like those
That walk in 'em, for so they did to me.
Look you, I told you truth: they're like a chain,
Draw but one link, all follows.

Enter HIPPOLITO *and* ISABELLA *the niece*

GUARDIANO   Oh affinity,
What piece of excellent workmanship art thou?   70
'Tis work clean wrought, for there's no lust, but love in't,
And that abundantly—when in stranger things,
There is no love at all, but what lust brings.

FABRITIO

On with your mask, for 'tis your part to see now,
And not be seen. Go to, make use of your time;   75
See what you mean to like—nay, and I charge you,
Like what you see. Do you hear me? there's no dallying.
The gentleman's almost twenty, and 'tis time
He were getting lawful heirs, and you a-breeding on 'em.

ISABELLA

Good father!

FABRITIO   Tell not me of tongues and rumours!   80
You'll say the gentleman is somewhat simple—
The better for a husband, were you wise:
For those that marry fools, live ladies' lives.
On with the mask, I'll hear no more; he's rich:
The fool's hid under bushels.

---

61 *stock . . . land.* Attempts were being made in the early 17th century to
    people Newfoundland; but the reference here is most probably to
    Virginia—as in Donne's Elegy: 'Oh my America, my new found lande'
    ('To his Mistris Going to Bed'). Middleton uses the same analogy in an
    earlier play: 'Take deliberation, sir; never choose a wife as if you were
    going to Virginia' (*The Roaring Girl*, II, ii, 71–2).
74–5 *On . . . seen.* In a contract like this, the man and woman might not
    see each other (officially at least) until the day of betrothal (see note at
    III, iii, 9–10).

LIVIA   Not so hid neither,   85
But here's a foul great piece of him, methinks:
What will he be, when he comes altogether?

Enter the WARD *with a trapstick, and* SORDIDO *his man*

WARD
Beat him?
I beat him out o'th'field with his own cat-stick,
Yet gave him the first hand.
SORDIDO   Oh strange!
WARD   I did it,   90
Then he set jacks on me.
SORDIDO   What, my lady's tailor?
WARD
Ay, and I beat him too.
SORDIDO   Nay, that's no wonder,
He's used to beating.
WARD   Nay, I tickled him
When I came once to my tippings.
SORDIDO   Now you talk on 'em,
there was a poulterer's wife made a great complaint of   95
you last night to your guardianer, that you struck a bump
in her child's head, as big as an egg.
WARD
An egg may prove a chicken, then in time the poulterer's
wife will get by't. When I am in game, I am furious; came
my mother's eyes in my way, I would not lose a fair end—   100
no, were she alive, but with one tooth in her head, I should
venture the striking out of that. I think of nobody, when
I am in play, I am so earnest. Coads me, my guardiner!
Prithee lay up my cat and cat-stick safe.

90 *first hand* first strike
91 *jacks* fellows

---

87 s.d. trapstick. A trapstick (or catstick) was used in the country game of
    tip-cat to strike the wooden cat (a short piece of wood tapered at both
    ends) so that it would fly in the air and then be struck again by the
    same player. The game is still played by schoolchildren in the north
    of England, who call it 'piggy'.
91 *my lady's tailor*. Tailors were popularly noted for their cowardice.
93 *beating*. Marlowe uses the same pun in *Dr Faustus*, where Wagner
    promises the Clown a whipping: he shall go 'in beaten silk' (I, iv, 15).
    Silk was embroidered by having gold and silver beaten into it.

SORDIDO

Where sir, i'th'chimney-corner?   105

WARD

Chimney-corner!

SORDIDO

Yes sir, your cats are always safe i'th'chimney-corner,
unless they burn their coats.

WARD

Marry, that I am afraid on.

SORDIDO

Why then, I will bestow your cat i'th'gutter, and there   110
she's safe, I am sure.

WARD

If I but live to keep a house, I'll make thee a great man—
if meat and drink can do't. I can stoop gallantly, and pitch
out when I list; I'm dog at a hole. I mar'l my guardiner
does not seek a wife for me; I protest, I'll have a bout with 115
the maids else, or contract myself at midnight to the
larder-woman in presence of a fool or a sack-posset.

GUARDIANO

Ward!

WARD

I feel myself after any exercise horribly prone: let me but
ride, I'm lusty—a cockhorse straight, i'faith.   120

105–30 *Where . . . cradle* (as verse O)
114 *mar'l* marvel
117 *sack-posset* beverage made with sack (dry wine), eggs and sugar
119 *prone* i.e. to lechery

105–8 *chimney-corner . . . coats.* Obscenity is to be expected from the Ward
and Sordido, but here it is obscured either by age or by imprecision.
Cat is a common term for 'whore'; and 'A young fellow falne in love
with a Whore, is said to be falne asleepe in the Chimney corner'
(Overbury, *Characters* (11th imp. 1623), V 1). *Burn* is the usual de-
scription of the action of syphilis: 'Bawds and Atturneys are Andyrons
that hold up their Clyents till they burne each other to ashes' (*ibid*, T 8ᵛ).
113 *stoop gallantly.* A dog picking up the scent is said to *stoop*, but Mulryne
has found a mention of the 'stoop gallant' or 'sweating sickness' (i.e.
venereal disease) in Nashe's *Pierce Peniless* (ed. McKerrow, iii, 114).
114 *dog at a hole.* A good hunter: 'I am dog at a catch' (*Twelfth Night*,
II, iii, 62). The Ward's train of thought makes the obscenity clear
enough.
117 *fool.* The fruit and cream dish may be meant, but 'fowl' could also be
intended, both here and at III, ii, 121. The homophony of *fool* and *fowl*
made a pun available: Daedalus 'taught his son the office of a fowl!
And yet, for all his wings, the fool was drown'd' (*3 Henry VI*, V, vi,
19–20).

GUARDIANO

Why, ward I say.

WARD

I'll forswear eating eggs in moon-shine nights; there's
nev'r a one I eat, but turns into a cock in four-and-twenty
hours; if my hot blood be not took down in time, sure
'twill crow shortly.   125

GUARDIANO

Do you hear, sir? follow me; I must new school you.

WARD

School me? I scorn that now; I am past schooling. I am
not so base to learn to write and read; I was born to better
fortunes in my cradle.

                    Exit [WARD, SORDIDO *and* GUARDIANO]

FABRITIO

How do you like him, girl? this is your husband.   130
Like him or like him not, wench, you shall have him,
And you shall love him.

LIVIA   Oh, soft there, brother!
Though you be a justice,
Your warrant cannot be served out of your liberty.
You may compel, out of the power of father,   135
Things merely harsh to a maid's flesh and blood;
But when you come to love, there the soil alters;
Y'are in another country, where your laws
Are no more set by, than the cacklings of geese
In Rome's great Capitol.

FABRITIO   Marry him she shall then;   140
Let her agree upon love afterwards.   *Exit*

LIVIA

You speak now, brother, like an honest mortal

134 *liberty* district with its own commission of peace

---

122 *eggs ... nights.* Eggs were said to be aphrodisiac: 'The very sight o
this egg has made him cockish' (Fletcher, *Women Pleased*, I, ii, 21).
Mulryne has suggested eggs-in-moonshine (poached eggs with onion
sauce, *O.E.D.* 3) as the proper collocation; but Middleton's fondness
for the phrase 'moonshine nights' (as at I, ii, 64) makes me prefer O's
punctuation.

128-9 *base ... cradle.* '... he can scarce write and read. He's the better
regarded for that amongst courtiers, for that's but a needy quality'
(*Michaelmas Term*, I, i, 305-7).

139-40 *cacklings ... Capitol.* Geese sacred to Juno were kept on the Capito-
line Hill, and on a famous occasion their cackling warned the Romans
of a surprise invasion by the Gauls. The comparison does not seem
particularly apt.

That walks upon th'earth with a staff;
You were up i'th'clouds before; you'ld command love—
And so do most old folks that go without it.   145
My best and dearest brother, I could dwell here;
There is not such another seat on earth
Where all good parts better express themselves.

HIPPOLITO
You'll make me blush anon.

LIVIA
'Tis but like saying grace before a feast, then,   150
And that's most comely; thou art all a feast,
And she that has thee, a most happy guest.
Prithee cheer up thy niece with special counsel.   [*Exit*]

HIPPOLITO
I would 'twere fit to speak to her what I would, but
'Twas not a thing ordained; Heaven has forbid it,   155
And 'tis most meet that I should rather perish
Than the decree divine receive least blemish.
Feed inward, you my sorrows, make no noise;
Consume me silent, let me be stark dead
Ere the world know I'm sick. You see my honesty,   160
If you befriend me—so.

ISABELLA   Marry a fool!
Can there be greater misery to a woman
That means to keep her days true to her husband,
And know no other man, so virtue wills it!
Why, how can I obey and honour him,   165
But I must needs commit idolatry?
A fool is but the image of a man,
And that but ill made neither. Oh the heartbreakings
Of miserable maids, where love's enforced!
The best condition is but bad enough: 170
When women have their choices, commonly
They do but buy their thraldoms, and bring great portions
To men to keep 'em in subjection:
As if a fearful prisoner should bribe
The keeper to be good to him, yet lies in still,   175
And glad of a good usage, a good look
Sometimes. By'r Lady, no misery surmounts a woman's!

153 *thy* ed (that O)
177 *Sometimes. By'r Lady, no* ed (Sometimes by'r Lady; no O)

---

146 *here.* Presumably Livia kisses Hippolito at this point.
166 *idolatry.* God created man in His own image; but a fool is the image of a
    man; therefore in promising to honour a fool, a woman commits idolatry.

Men buy their slaves, but women buy their masters.
Yet honesty and love makes all this happy
And, next to angels', the most blest estate.   180
That Providence, that has made ev'ry poison
Good for some use, and sets four warring elements
At peace in man, can make a harmony
In things that are most strange to human reason.
Oh but this marriage! What, are you sad too, uncle?   185
'Faith, then there's a whole household down together:
Where shall I go to seek my comfort now
When my best friend's distressed? What is't afflicts you, sir?

HIPPOLITO
'Faith, nothing but one grief that will not leave me,
And now 'tis welcome; ev'ry man has something   190
To bring him to his end, and this will serve,
Joined with your father's cruelty to you—
That helps it forward.

ISABELLA   Oh be cheered, sweet uncle!
How long has't been upon you? I nev'r spied it;
What a dull sight have I! how long, I pray sir?   195

HIPPOLITO
Since I first saw you, niece, and left Bologna.

ISABELLA
And could you deal so unkindly with my heart,
To keep it up so long hid from my pity?
Alas, how shall I trust your love hereafter!
Have we passed through so many arguments,   200
And missed of that still, the most needful one?
Walked out whole nights together in discourses,
And the main point forgot? We are too blame both;
This is an obstinate wilful forgetfulness,
And faulty on both parts. Let's lose no time now.   205
Begin, good uncle, you that feel't; what is it?

HIPPOLITO
You of all creatures, niece, must never hear on't;
'Tis not a thing ordained for you to know.

ISABELLA
Not I, sir! all my joys that word cuts off;

181-2 *poison . . . use*. 'No poison, sir, but serves us for some use' (*The
    Roaring Girl*, IV, i, 151).
182 *four . . . elements*. Four elements made up the world (in the Ptolemaic
    system) and also the little world of man, in which they strove continually
    for dominance over the personality: 'Nature, that fram'd us of four
    elements Warring within our breasts for regiment' (Marlowe, *1 Tam-
    burlaine*, II, vii, 18-19).

You made profession once you loved me best—   210
'Twas but profession!

HIPPOLITO   Yes, I do't too truly,
And fear I shall be chid for't. Know the worst then:
I love thee dearlier than an uncle can.

ISABELLA
Why, so you ever said, and I believed it.

HIPPOLITO
So simple is the goodness of her thoughts   215
They understand not yet th'unhallowed language
Of a near sinner: I must yet be forced
(Though blushes be my venture) to come nearer.
As a man loves his wife, so love I thee.

ISABELLA   What's that?
Methought I heard ill news come toward me,   220
Which commonly we understand too soon,
Than over-quick at hearing. I'll prevent it,
Though my joys fare the harder; welcome it—
It shall nev'r come so near mine ear again.
Farewell all friendly solaces and discourses;   225
I'll learn to live without ye, for your dangers
Are greater than your comforts. What's become
Of truth in love, if such we cannot trust.
When blood that should be love is mixed with lust!   *Exit*

HIPPOLITO
The worst can be but death, and let it come;   230
He that lives joyless, every day's his doom.   *Exit*

Act I, Scene iii

Enter LEANTIO *alone*

LEANTIO
Methinks I'm ev'n as dull now at departure
As men observe great gallants the next day
After a revels; you shall see 'em look
Much of my fashion, if you mark 'em well.

217 *near.* The first of several uses of this word which bring into play multiple
     meanings—here 'almost a sinner' and 'a closely related sinner'.
220–24 *Methought ... again.* The sense of this is difficult to make out.
     Isabella seems to be saying that trouble is more readily apprehended
     intuitively ('we understand') than intellectually (by 'hearing') and that,
     having grasped her uncle's meaning from his stammered phrases, she
     will not wait for a fuller explanation but will anticipate ('prevent') the
     bad news; in thus meeting it ('welcome it') she will stop him from
     speaking further.

'Tis ev'n a second hell to part from pleasure   5
When man has got a smack on't. As many holidays
Coming together makes your poor heads idle
A great while after, and are said to stick
Fast in their fingers' ends; ev'n so does game
In a new-married couple for the time;   10
It spoils all thrift, and indeed lies a-bed

          [*Enter*] BIANCA *and* MOTHER *above*

To invent all the new ways for great expenses.
See, and she be not got on purpose now
Into the window to look after me!
I have no power to go now and I should be hanged.   15
Farewell all business! I desire no more
Than I see yonder. Let the goods at quay
Look to themselves; why should I toil my youth out?
It is but begging two or three year sooner,
And stay with her continually: is't a match?   20
Oh fie, what a religion have I leaped into!
Get out again, for shame! The man loves best
When his care's most—that shows his zeal to love.
Fondness is but the idiot to affection,
That plays at hot-cockles with rich merchants' wives;   25
Good to make sport withal when the chest's full,
And the long warehouse cracks. 'Tis time of day
For us to be more wise; 'tis early with us,
And if they lose the morning of their affairs
They commonly lose the best part of the day.   30
Those that are wealthy and have got enough,
'Tis after sunset with 'em; they may rest,
Grow fat with ease, banquet, and toy and play,
When such as I enter the heat o'th'day;
And I'll do't cheerfully.
BIANCA   I perceive, sir,   35
Y'are not gone yet; I have good hope you'll stay now.

---

6 *smack* taste   15 *and* if

8–9 *stick . . . ends*. This sounds proverbial; or it may be a variant on the
expression 'to have something at one's fingertips'.
24–5 *Fondness . . . wives*. Infatuation ('Fondness') is a fool ('idiot') compared to real love and serves only to titillate rich women.
25 *hot-cockles*. Literally, a country game similar to blind man's buff; by
frequent application it comes to refer also to sexual play.
29–30 *lose . . . day*. Proverbial: 'He who sleeps all the morning may go a
begging all the day after' (Tilley, M 1172).

LEANTIO
   Farewell, I must not.
BIANCA   Come, come; pray return.
   Tomorrow, adding but a little care more,
   Will dispatch all as well—believe me, 'twill sir.
LEANTIO
   I could well wish myself where you would have me;   40
   But love that's wanton must be ruled awhile
   By that that's careful, or all goes to ruin.
   As fitting is a government in love
   As in a kingdom; where 'tis all mere lust
   'Tis like an insurrection in the people   45
   That, raised in self-will, wars against all reason:
   But love that is respective of increase
   Is like a good king, that keeps all in peace.
   Once more, farewell.
BIANCA   But this one night, I prithee.
LEANTIO
   Alas, I'm in for twenty, if I stay,   50
   And then for forty more, I have such luck to flesh:
   I never bought a horse, but he bore double.
   If I stay any longer, I shall turn
   An everlasting spendthrift; as you love
   To be maintained well, do not call me again,   55
   For then I shall not care which end goes forward.
   Again, farewell to thee.   *Exit*
BIANCA   Since it must, farewell too.
MOTHER
   'Faith daughter, y'are too blame; you take the course
   To make him an ill husband, troth you do,
   And that disease is catching, I can tell you—   60
   Ay, and soon taken by a young man's blood,
   And that with little urging. Nay, fie, see now—

47 *respective of* careful for

43–5 *government . . . people.* Leantio makes the stock Elizabethan comparison
   between the individual (here, the lovers) and the body politic: '. . . the
   state of man, Like to a little kingdom, suffers then The nature of an
   insurrection' (*Julius Caesar*, II, i, 67–9).
48 *good king . . . peace.* Jacobean dramatists were often careful to introduce
   flattery of James the peacemaker into their plays. Middleton shows
   more discrimination in this than the sometimes sycophantic Massinger
   (cf. the character of Roberto in *The Maid of Honour*).
56 *care . . . forward.* Proverbial: 'He cares not which end goes forward'
   (Tilley, E 130).

What cause have you to weep? would I had no more,
That have lived threescore years; there were a cause
And 'twere well thought on. Trust me, y'are too blame;   65
His absence cannot last five days at utmost.
Why should those tears be fetched forth? cannot love
Be ev'n as well expressed in a good look,
But it must see her face still in a fountain?
It shows like a country maid dressing her head   70
By a dish of water. Come, 'tis an old custom
To weep for love.

Enter two or three BOYS, *and a* CITIZEN *or two, with an*
APPRENTICE

BOYS
Now they come! now they come!
2 BOY   The duke!
3 BOY   The state!
CITIZEN
How near, boy?
1 BOY   I'th'next street sir, hard at hand.
CITIZEN
You sirra, get a standing for your mistress,   75
The best in all the city.
APPRENTICE   I have't for her, sir.
'Twas a thing I provided for her over-night,
'Tis ready at her pleasure.
CITIZEN
Fetch her to't then; away sir!
BIANCA
What's the meaning of this hurry,   80
Can you tell, mother?
MOTHER   What a memory
Have I! I see by that years come upon me.
Why, 'tis a yearly custom and solemnity,
Religiously observed by th'duke and state,
To St Mark's temple, the fifteenth of April.   85
See if my dull brains had not quite forgot it!
'Twas happily questioned of thee; I had gone down else,
Sat like a drone below, and never thought on't.

83 *solemnity* festival

---

85 *the fifteenth of April.* The Feast of St Mark, when this procession
(according to Moryson) took place, is 25 April. Perhaps Middleton,
neither chronologist nor hagiolater, arrived at his date simply by
subtracting the ten days by which the English (Julian) calendar was
behind the continental (Gregorian).

I would not to be ten years younger again
That you had lost the sight; now you shall see   90
Our duke, a goodly gentleman of his years.
BIANCA
Is he old then?
MOTHER   About some fifty-five.
BIANCA
That's no great age in man; he's then at best
For wisdom and for judgement.
MOTHER   The lord cardinal,
His noble brother—there's a comely gentleman,   95
And greater in devotion than in blood.
BIANCA
He's worthy to be marked.
MOTHER   You shall behold
All our chief states of Florence; you came fortunately
Against this solemn day.
BIANCA   I hope so always.   *Music*
MOTHER
I hear 'em near us now; do you stand easily?   100
BIANCA
Exceeding well, good mother.
MOTHER   Take this stool.
BIANCA
I need it not, I thank you.
MOTHER   Use your will, then.

Enter in great solemnity six KNIGHTS *bare-headed, then two*
CARDINALS, *and then the* LORD CARDINAL, *then the* DUKE; *after
him the* STATES *of* FLORENCE *by two and two, with variety of
music and song*

                                                      Exit

MOTHER
How like you, daughter?
BIANCA   'Tis a noble state.
Methinks my soul could dwell upon the reverence
Of such a solemn and most worthy custom.   105
Did not the duke look up? me-thought he saw us.
MOTHER
That's everyone's conceit that sees a duke:
If he look steadfastly, he looks straight at them—
When he perhaps, good careful gentleman,
Never minds any, but the look he casts   110
Is at his own intentions, and his object
Only the public good.

BIANCA   Most likely so.
MOTHER
Come, come, we'll end this argument below.   *Exeunt*

Act II, Scene i

Enter HIPPOLITO *and* LADY LIVIA *the widow*

LIVIA
A strange affection, brother, when I think on't!
I wonder how thou cam'st by't.
HIPPOLITO   Ev'n as easily
As man comes by destruction, which oft-times
He wears in his own bosom.
LIVIA   Is the world
So populous in women, and creation   5
So prodigal in beauty and so various,
Yet does love turn thy point to thine own blood?
'Tis somewhat too unkindly. Must thy eye
Dwell evilly on the fairness of thy kindred,
And seek not where it should? It is confined   10
Now in a narrower prison than was made for't:
It is allowed a stranger; and where bounty
Is made the great man's honour, 'tis ill husbandry
To spare, and servants shall have small thanks for't.
So he Heaven's bounty seems to scorn and mock,   15
That spares free means, and spends of his own stock.
HIPPOLITO
Never was man's misery so soon sewed up,
Counting how truly.
LIVIA   Nay, I love you so,
That I shall venture much to keep a change from you
So fearful as this grief will bring upon you—   20
'Faith, it even kills me, when I see you faint
Under a reprehension; and I'll leave it,
Though I know nothing can be better for you.

17 *sewed* ed (sow'd O; summ'd Bullen); *sow* is a regular variant for
   sew
19 *venture* hazard
22 *reprehension* reprimand

2–4 *Ev'n . . . bosom.* 'See, sin needs No other destruction than [what] it
   breeds In its own bosom' (Middleton, *The Mayor of Queenborough*,
   V, ii, 76–8).
8 *unkindly.* With a pun (again, the first of many) on *kin/kind*: 'A little
   more than kin and less than kind' (*Hamlet*, I, ii, 65).

Prithee, sweet brother, let not passion waste
The goodness of thy time, and of thy fortune; 25
Thou keep'st the treasure of that life I love
As dearly as mine own; and if you think
My former words too bitter, which were ministered
By truth and zeal—'tis but a hazarding
Of grace and virtue, and I can bring forth 30
As pleasant fruits as sensuality wishes
In all her teeming longings. This I can do.

HIPPOLITO
Oh nothing that can make my wishes perfect!

LIVIA
I would that love of yours were pawned to't, brother,
And as soon lost that way as I could win. 35
Sir, I could give as shrewd a lift to chastity
As any she that wears a tongue in Florence:
Sh'ad need be a good horsewoman and sit fast
Whom my strong argument could not fling at last.
Prithee take courage, man; though I should counsel 40
Another to despair, yet I am pitiful
To thy afflictions, and will venture hard—
I will not name for what, 'tis not handsome;
Find you the proof, and praise me.

HIPPOLITO   Then I fear me,
I shall not praise you in haste.

LIVIA   This is the comfort, 45
You are not the first, brother, has attempted
Things more forbidden than this seems to be.
I'll minister all cordials now to you,
Because I'll cheer you up, sir.

HIPPOLITO   I am past hope.

LIVIA
Love, thou shalt see me do a strange cure then, 50

36 *give . . . a lift to* attack

26-7 *love . . . own.* In the source the nun tells Hipolito that what he needs
'is the advice of a faithfull friend, and where can you expect it more
faithfull, then from me, who you know have not onely loved you above
my other Brothers, but even before my selfe' (*Hipolito & Isabella*,
pp. 27-8).

37 *any . . . tongue.* Any articulate woman; but jewellery in the shape of
tongues was popular at this time: the king in Marlowe's *Edward II*
promises to 'hang a golden tongue' about his wife's neck (I, iv, 327).

46-7 *You . . . be.* The nun comforts Hipolito: 'You are not the first that
have undertaken things as much forbidden, which have yet attained to a
happie end' (*Hipolito & Isabella*, p. 33).

As e'er was wrought on a disease so mortal
And near akin to shame. When shall you see her?

HIPPOLITO
Never in comfort more.

LIVIA   Y'are so impatient too.

HIPPOLITO
Will you believe—'death, sh'as forsworn my company,
And sealed it with a blush.

LIVIA   So, I perceive   55
All lies upon my hands, then; well, the more glory
When the work's finished.

Enter SERVANT

                    How now, sir, the news?

SERVANT
Madam, your niece, the virtuous Isabella,
Is lighted now to see you.

LIVIA   That's great fortune.
Sir, your stars bless you simply. Lead her in.   60
                                        Exit SERVANT

HIPPOLITO
What's this to me?

LIVIA   Your absence, gentle brother;
I must bestir my wits for you.

HIPPOLITO   Ay, to great purpose.
                                        Exit HIPPOLITO

LIVIA
Beshrew you, would I loved you not so well!
I'll go to bed, and leave this deed undone;
I am the fondest where I once affect,   65
The carefull'st of their healths, and of their ease, forsooth,
That I look still but slenderly to mine own.
I take a course to pity him so much now,
That I have none left for modesty and myself.
This 'tis to grow so liberal—y'have few sisters   70
That love their brother's ease 'bove their own honesties:
But if you question my affections,
That will be found my fault.

---

54 *'death* by God's death   65 *fondest* most foolish

---

60 *bless you simply. Lead* Ed (bless, you simple, lead O; bless you.—Simple,
lead Dyce; bless you; you simple, lead Simpson). I am not happy about
the addressing of a servant as *Simple*, or even as *you simple*, and so have
emended to *simply* which I take to mean 'richly, abundantly' as at
IV, i, 43.

Enter ISABELLA *the niece*

　　　　　　　　　　　Niece, your love's welcome.
Alas, what draws that paleness to thy cheeks?
This enforced marriage towards?
ISABELLA　　　　　　　　　It helps, good aunt,　　75
Amongst some other griefs—but those I'll keep
Locked up in modest silence; for they're sorrows
Would shame the tongue more than they grieve the thought.

LIVIA
Indeed, the ward is simple.
ISABELLA　　　　　　Simple! that were well:
Why, one might make good shift with such a husband.　　80
But he's a fool entailed, he halts downright in't.

LIVIA
And knowing this, I hope 'tis at your choice
To take or refuse, niece.
ISABELLA　　　　　You see it is not.
I loathe him more than beauty can hate death,
Or age, her spiteful neighbour.
LIVIA　　　　　　　　　Let 't appear, then.　　85

ISABELLA
How can I, being born with that obedience
That must submit unto a father's will?
If he command, I must of force consent.

LIVIA
Alas, poor soul! Be not offended, prithee,
If I set by the name of niece awhile,　　90
And bring in pity in a stranger fashion.
It lies here in this breast, would cross this match.

ISABELLA
How, cross it, aunt?
LIVIA　　　　　　Ay, and give thee more liberty
Than thou hast reason yet to apprehend.

ISABELLA
Sweet aunt, in goodness keep not hid from me　　95
What may befriend my life.
LIVIA　　　　　　Yes, yes, I must,
When I return to reputation,
And think upon the solemn vow I made
To your dead mother, my most loving sister . . .

---

75 *towards* approaching
81 *entailed* indissolubly
81 *halts . . . in't* stops completely at this　　88 *of force* of necessity
94 *apprehend* understand　　　　99 *sister* sister-in-law, to be exact

As long as I have her memory 'twixt mine eyelids,   100
Look for no pity, now.

ISABELLA   Kind, sweet, dear aunt—

LIVIA

No, 'twas a secret I have took special care of,
Delivered by your mother on her deathbed—
That's nine years now—and I'll not part from 't yet,
Though nev'r was fitter time nor greater cause for 't.   105

ISABELLA

As you desire the praises of a virgin—

LIVIA

Good sorrow! I would do thee any kindness,
Not wronging secrecy or reputation . . .

ISABELLA

Neither of which, as I have hope of fruit[ful]ness,
Shall receive wrong from me.

LIVIA   Nay, 'twould be your own
                                          wrong 110
As much as any's, should it come to that once.

ISABELLA

I need no better means to work persuasion then.

LIVIA

Let it suffice, you may refuse this fool,
Or you may take him, as you see occasion
For your advantage: the best wits will do't.   115
Y'have liberty enough in your own will;
You cannot be enforced—there grows the flower,
If you could pick it out, makes whole life sweet to you.
That which you call your father's command's nothing:
Then your obedience must needs be as little.   120
If you can make shift here to taste your happiness,
Or pick out aught that likes you, much good do you.
You see your cheer, I'll make you no set dinner.

ISABELLA

And trust me, I may starve for all the good
I can find yet in this! Sweet aunt, deal plainlier.   125

LIVIA

Say I should trust you now upon an oath,
And give you in a secret that would start you;
How am I sure of you, in faith and silence?

ISABELLA

Equal assurance may I find in mercy,
As you for that in me.

---

109 *hope of fruit[ful]ness.* (fruitness O): 'By my hope of fruitfulness' (Middleton, *More Dissemblers Besides Women*, II, iii, 54).

LIVIA   It shall suffice.   130
  Then know, however custom has made good,
  For reputation's sake, the names of niece
  And aunt 'twixt you and I, w'are nothing less.
ISABELLA
  How's that!
LIVIA   I told you I should start your blood.
  You are no more allied to any of us,   135
  Save what the courtesy of opinion casts
  Upon your mother's memory and your name,
  Than the mer'st stranger is, or one begot
  At Naples when the husband lies at Rome;
  There's so much odds betwixt us. Since your knowledge   140
  Wished more instruction, and I have your oath
  In pledge for silence, it makes me talk the freelier.
  Did never the report of that famed Spaniard,
  Marquess of Coria, since your time was ripe
  For understanding, fill your ear with wonder?   145
ISABELLA
  Yes, what of him? I have heard his deeds of honour
  Often related when we lived in Naples.
LIVIA
  You heard the praises of your father then.
ISABELLA
  My father!
LIVIA   That was he; but all the business
  So carefully and so discreetly carried   150
  That fame received no spot by't, not a blemish.
  Your mother was so wary to her end;
  None knew it but her conscience, and her friend,
  Till penitent confession made it mine,
  And now my pity, yours: it had been long else,   155
  And I hope care and love alike in you,
  Made good by oath, will see it take no wrong now.
  How weak his commands now, whom you call father?
  How vain all his enforcements, your obedience?
  And what a largeness in your will and liberty   160
  To take or to reject—or to do both?
  For fools will serve to father wise men's children—
  All this y'have time to think on. Oh my wench,
  Nothing o'erthrows our sex but indiscretion!
  We might do well else of a brittle people   165

---

164 *Nothing . . . indiscretion.* 'Neece (answered the Nunne) nothing undoth
  us but indiscretion' (*Hipolito & Isabella*, p. 46).

As any under the great canopy.
I pray forget not but to call me aunt still—
Take heed of that, it may be marked in time else.
But keep your thoughts to yourself, from all the world,
Kindred or dearest friend—nay, I entreat you,   170
From him that all this while you have called uncle;
And though you love him dearly, as I know
His deserts claim as much ev'n from a stranger,
Yet let not him know this, I prithee do not;
As ever thou hast hope of second pity   175
If thou shouldst stand in need on't, do not do't.

ISABELLA
Believe my oath, I will not.

LIVIA   Why, well said.
—Who shows more craft t'undo a maidenhead,
I'll resign my part to her.

Enter HIPPOLITO

                        She's thine own, go.   *Exit*

HIPPOLITO
Alas, fair flattery cannot cure my sorrows!   180

ISABELLA
Have I passed so much time in ignorance,
And never had the means to know myself
Till this blest hour! Thanks to her virtuous pity
That brought it now to light—would I had known it
But one day sooner! he had then received   185
In favours what, poor gentleman, he took
In bitter words—a slight and harsh reward
For one of his deserts.

HIPPOLITO   There seems to me now
More anger and distraction in her looks.
I'm gone, I'll not endure a second storm;   190
The memory of the first is not past yet.

ISABELLA
Are you returned, you comforts of my life,
In this man's presence? I will keep you fast now,
And sooner part eternally from the world
Than my good joys in you. Prithee, forgive me.   195
I did but chide in jest; the best loves use it
Sometimes; it sets an edge upon affection.
When we invite our best friends to a feast
'Tis not all sweetmeats that we set before them,

---

166 *great canopy.* The firmament: 'This most excellent canopy the air, look
   you, this brave o'erhanging' (*Hamlet*, II, ii, 14).

There's somewhat sharp and salt, both to whet appetite,   200
And make 'em taste their wine well: so, methinks,
After a friendly, sharp, and savoury chiding,
A kiss tastes wondrous well and full o'th'grape—
                                        [*kisses him*]
—How think'st thou, does't not?
HIPPOLITO   'Tis so excellent,
I know not how to praise it, what to say to't!   205
ISABELLA
This marriage shall go forward.
HIPPOLITO   With the ward!
Are you in earnest?
ISABELLA   'Twould be ill for us else.
HIPPOLITO
For us! how means she that?
ISABELLA   Troth, I begin
To be so well, methinks, within this hour—
For all this match able to kill one's heart—   210
Nothing can pull me down now; should my father
Provide a worse fool yet (which I should think
Were a hard thing to compass) I'ld have him either:
The worse the better; none can come amiss now
If he want wit enough. So discretion love me,   215
Desert and judgement, I have content sufficient.
She that comes once to be a housekeeper
Must not look every day to fare well, sir,
Like a young waiting gentlewoman in service;
For she feeds commonly as her lady does,   220
No good bit passes her but she gets a taste on't;
But when she comes to keep house for herself,
She's glad of some choice cates then once a week,
Or twice at most, and glad if she can get 'em:
So must affection learn to fare with thankfulness.   225
Pray make your love no stranger, sir, that's all.
—Though you be one yourself, and know not on't,
And I have sworn you must not.   *Exit*
HIPPOLITO   This is beyond me!
Never came joys so unexpectedly
To meet desires in man. How came she thus?   230
What has she done to her, can any tell?
'Tis beyond sorcery, this, drugs or love-powders;
Some art that has no name, sure; strange to me
Of all the wonders I ere met withal

223 *cates* delicacies

Throughout my ten years' travels. But I'm thankful for't.   235
This marriage now must of necessity forward:
It is the only veil wit can devise
To keep our acts hid from sin-piercing eyes.   *Exit*

Act II, Scene ii

Enter GUARDIANO *and* LIVIA

LIVIA
How, sir, a gentlewoman so young, so fair,
As you set forth, spied from the widow's window?
GUARDIANO
She!
LIVIA
Our Sunday-dinner woman?
GUARDIANO
And Thursday-supper woman, the same still.   5
I know not how she came by her, but I'll swear
She's the prime gallant for a face in Florence,
And no doubt other parts follow their leader.
The duke himself first spied her at the window,
Then in a rapture, as if admiration   10
Were poor when it were single, beckoned me,
And pointed to the wonder warily,
As one that feared she would draw in her splendour
Too soon, if too much gazed at. I nev'r knew him
So infinitely taken with a woman;   15
Nor can I blame his appetite, or tax
His raptures of slight folly; she's a creature
Able to draw a state from serious business,
And make it their best piece to do her service.
What course shall we devise? h'as spoke twice now.   20
LIVIA
Twice?
GUARDIANO 'Tis beyond your apprehension
How strangely that one look has catched his heart!
'Twould prove but too much worth in wealth and favour
To those should work his peace.
LIVIA   And if I do't not,
Or at least come as near it (if your art   25
Will take a little pains and second me)
As any wench in Florence of my standing,
I'll quite give o'er, and shut up shop in cunning.

22 *strangely* ed (strangly O)

GUARDIANO

'Tis for the duke; and if I fail your purpose,
All means to come, by riches or advancement,   30
Miss me and skip me over!

LIVIA   Let the old woman then
Be sent for with all speed; then I'll begin.

GUARDIANO

A good conclusion follow, and a sweet one,
After this stale beginning with old ware.
Within there!

Enter SERVANT

SERVANT   Sir, do you call?

GUARDIANO   Come near, list hither.   35

LIVIA

I long myself to see this absolute creature
That wins the heart of love and praise so much.

GUARDIANO

Go sir, make haste.

LIVIA   Say I entreat her company;
Do you hear, sir?

SERVANT   Yes, madam.   *Exit*

LIVIA   That brings her quickly.

GUARDIANO

I would 'twere done; the duke waits the good hour,   40
And I wait the good fortune that may spring from't:
I have had a lucky hand these fifteen year
At such court-passage with three dice in a dish.

Enter FABRITIO

Signor Fabritio!

ABRITIO

Oh sir, I bring an alteration in my mouth now.   45

GUARDIANO

An alteration! no wise speech, I hope;
He means not to talk wisely does he, trow?
Good! what's the change, I pray sir?

FABRITIO   A new change.

GUARDIANO

Another yet! 'faith, there's enough already.

---

43 *court-passage.* '*Passage* is a Game at Dice to be play'd at but by two, and
it is performed with three Dice. The *Caster* throws continually till he
hath thrown Doublets under ten, and then he is out and loseth; or
doublets above ten, and then he *passeth* and wins' (Charles Cotton,
The Compleat Gamester (1674), p. 167).

FABRITIO
　My daughter loves him now.

GUARDIANO　　　　　　　　　　What, does she, sir?　　　　50

FABRITIO
　Affects him beyond thought—who but the ward, forsooth!
　No talk but of the ward; she would have him
　To choose 'bove all the men she ever saw.
　My will goes not so fast as her consent now;
　Her duty gets before my command still.　　　　55

GUARDIANO
　Why then sir, if you'll have me speak my thoughts,
　I smell 'twill be a match.

FABRITIO　　　　　　　　Ay, and a sweet young couple,
　If I have any judgement.

GUARDIANO　　　　　　　　—'Faith, that's little.
　Let her be sent tomorrow before noon,
　And handsomely tricked up, for 'bout that time　　　　60
　I mean to bring her in and tender her to him.

FABRITIO
　I warrant you for handsome; I will see
　Her things laid ready, every one in order,
　And have some part of her tricked up tonight.

GUARDIANO
　Why, well said.

FABRITIO　　　　　'Twas a use her mother had　　　　65
　When she was invited to an early wedding;
　She'ld dress her head o'ernight, sponge up herself,
　And give her neck three lathers.

GUARDIANO　　　　　　　　　Ne'er a halter?

FABRITIO
　On with her chain of pearl, her ruby bracelets,
　Lay ready all her tricks and jiggambobs.　　　　70

GUARDIANO
　So must your daughter.

FABRITIO　　　　　　　I'll about it straight, sir.

　　　　　　　　　　　　　　　　　Exit FABRITIO

LIVIA
　How he sweats in the foolish zeal of fatherhood
　After six ounces an hour, and seems
　To toil as much as if his cares were wise ones!

GUARDIANO
　Y'have let his folly blood in the right vein, lady.　　　　75

---

　68 *lathers . . . halter*. The *halter* would be made of leather—for which
　　lather is a variant form.

LIVIA

And here comes his sweet son-in-law that shall be.
They're both allied in wit before the marriage;
What will they be hereafter, when they are nearer?
Yet they can go no further than the fool:
There's the word's end in both of 'em.

Enter WARD *and* SORDIDO, *one with a shuttlecock, the
other a battledore*

GUARDIANO   Now, young heir!   80
WARD

What's the next business after shuttlecock, now?

GUARDIANO

Tomorrow you shall see the gentlewoman must be your
wife.

WARD

There's ev'n another thing too must be kept up with a
pair of battledores. My wife! what can she do?   85

GUARDIANO

Nay, that's a question you should ask yourself, ward,
when y'are alone together.

WARD

That's as I list! A wife's to be asked anywhere, I hope;
I'll ask her in a congregation, if I have a mind to't, and
so save a licence.—My guardiner has no more wit than an   90
herb-woman, that sells away all her sweet herbs and
nosegays, and keeps a stinking breath for her own pottage.

SORDIDO

Let me be at the choosing of your beloved, if you desire a
woman of good parts.

WARD

Thou shalt, sweet Sordido.   95

SORDIDO

I have a plaguey guess; let me alone to see what she is.

---

80 *word's* ed (worlds O)
82–9 *Tomorrow . . . hope* (as verse O)   88 *asked* ed (ask O)

84–5 *kept . . . battledores.* The Ward's intention is obscene—although
again obscurely so. Isabella for the banquet has 'a lusty sprouting sprig
in her hair' (III, ii, 14), and perhaps Middleton is thinking of her as one
of the harlots he describes in *Father Hubburd's Tales*: 'such shuttlecocks
as these, which, though they are tossed and played withal, go still like
maids, all white on top' (viii, 79).
89–90 *ask . . . licence.* Unless the banns of marriage were publicly pro-
claimed in church ('congregation') a special licence was necessary.

If I but look upon her—'way, I know all the faults to a
hair that you may refuse her for.

WARD

Dost thou? I prithee let me hear 'em Sordido.

SORDIDO

Well, mark 'em then; I have 'em all in rhyme.   100
 The wife your guardiner ought to tender,
 Should be pretty, straight and slender;
 Her hair not short, her foot not long,
 Her hand not huge, nor too too loud her tongue;
 No pearl in eye nor ruby in her nose,   105
 No burn or cut but what the catalogue shows.
 She must have teeth, and that no black ones,
 And kiss most sweet when she does smack once:
 Her skin must be both white and plumpt,
 Her body straight, not hopper-rumped,   110
 Or wriggle sideways like a crab.
 She must be neither slut nor drab,
 Nor go too splay-foot with her shoes
 To make her smock lick up the dews.
 And two things more which I forgot to tell ye: 115
 She neither must have bump in back nor belly.
 These are the faults that will not make her pass.

WARD

 And if I spy not these I am a rank ass!

SORDIDO

Nay, more—by right, sir, you should see her naked,
For that's the ancient order.

WARD   See her naked?   120
That were good sport, i'faith. I'll have the books turned over,
And if I find her naked on record
She shall not have a rag on—but stay, stay!
How if she should desire to see me so too?
I were in a sweet case then; such a foul skin!   125

_____

109 *plumpt* ed (plump O)

_____

105 *pearl in eye.* The whitish spot in the eye left by certain diseases (such as
 smallpox): 'A pearl in mine eye! I thank you for that; do you wish me
 blind?' (Middleton, *The Spanish Gipsy*, II, i, 167–8).
110 *hopper-rumped.* The hopper of a mill is shaped like an inverted pyramid
 and has a hopping or shaking movement.
119 *see her naked.* It was a Utopian custom: 'For a sad and honest matrone
 sheweth the woman, be she mayde or widdowe, naked to the wower.
 And lykewyse a sage and discrete man exhibyteth the wower naked to
 the woman' (More, *Utopia* (ed. Arber, 1869), p. 123).

SORDIDO
    But y'have a clean shirt, and that makes amends, sir.
WARD
    I will not see her naked for that trick, though.
SORDIDO
    Then take her with all faults with her clothes on,
    And they may hide a number with a bum-roll.
    'Faith, choosing of a wench in a huge farthingale   130
    Is like the buying of ware under a great penthouse:
    What with the deceit of one,
    And the false light of th'other, mark my speeches,
    He may have a diseased wench in's bed
    And rotten stuff in's breeches.   *Exit*   135
GUARDIANO
    It may take handsomely.
LIVIA   I see small hindrance.
    How now, so soon returned?

                    Enter [SERVANT *with*] MOTHER

GUARDIANO   She's come.
LIVIA   That's well.
    Widow, come, come; I have a great quarrel to you,
    'Faith, I must chide you, that you must be sent for!
    You make yourself so strange, never come at us,   140
    And yet so near a neighbour, and so unkind!
    Troth, y'are too blame; you cannot be more welcome
    To any house in Florence, that I'll tell you.
MOTHER
    My thanks must needs acknowledge so much, madam.
LIVIA
    How can you be so strange then? I sit here   145
    Sometime whole days together without company
    When business draws this gentleman from home,
    And should be happy in society
    Which I so well affect as that of yours.
    I know y'are alone too; why should not we,   150
    Like two kind neighbours, then, supply the wants

---

129 *bum-roll* cushion to hold out the full skirt

---

130 *choosing . . . farthingale.* '. . . wires and tires, bents and bums, felts and
    falls, thou that shalt deceive the world, that gentlewomen indeed shall
    not be known from others' (*Michaelmas Term*, I, ii, 13–15).
133 *false light.* 'My shop is not altogether so dark as some of my neighbours',
    where a man may be made cuckold at one end, while he's measuring
    with his yard at t'other' (*Michaelmas Term*, II, iii, 34–7).

Of one another, having tongue-discourse,
Experience in the world, and such kind helps
To laugh down time, and meet age merrily?

MOTHER
Age, madam! you speak mirth; 'tis at my door,   155
But a long journey from your ladyship yet.

LIVIA
My faith, I'm nine-and-thirty, ev'ry stroke, wench;
And 'tis a general observation
'Mongst knights: wives or widows, we account
Ourselves then old, when young men's eyes leave looking at's: 160
'Tis a true rule amongst us, and ne'er failed yet
In any but in one that I remember;
Indeed, she had a friend at nine-and-forty!
—Marry, she paid well for him; and in th'end
He kept a quean or two with her own money,   165
That robbed her of her plate and cut her throat.

MOTHER
She had her punishment in this world, madam;
And a fair warning to all other women
That they live chaste at fifty.

LIVIA   Ay, or never, wench.
Come, now I have thy company I'll not part with't   170
Till after supper.

MOTHER   Yes, I must crave pardon, madam.

LIVIA
I swear you shall stay supper; we have no strangers, woman,
None but my sojourners and I—this gentleman
And the young heir, his ward. You know our company.

MOTHER
Some other time I will make bold with you, madam.   175

GUARDIANO
Nay, pray stay widow.

LIVIA   'Faith, she shall not go.
Do you think I'll be forsworn?   *Table and chess*

MOTHER   'Tis a great while
Till supper-time; I'll take my leave, then, now madam,
And come again i'th'evening, since your ladyship
Will have it so.

LIVIA   I'th'evening! By my troth, wench,   180

---

173 *sojourners* lodgers

---

177 s.d. Table and chess. O retains the prompt-book's warning of properties
    that will be needed shortly.

I'll keep you while I have you; you have great business, sure,
To sit alone at home. I wonder strangely
What pleasure you take in't! were't to me now,
I should be ever at one neighbour's house
Or other all day long, having no charge,   185
Or none to chide you if you go or stay.
Who may live merrier—ay, or more at heart's ease?
Come, we'll to chess or draughts; there are an hundred tricks
To drive out time till supper, never fear't, wench.

MOTHER
I'll but make one step home and return straight, madam.   190

LIVIA
Come, I'll not trust you; you use more excuses
To your kind friends than ever I knew any.
What business can you have, if you be sure
Y'have locked the doors? and that being all you have,
I know y'are careful on't. One afternoon   195
So much to spend here! say I should entreat you now
To lie a night or two, or a week, with me,
Or leave your own house for a month together—
It were a kindness that long neighbourhood
And friendship might well hope to prevail in—   200
Would you deny such a request? i'faith,
Speak truth, and freely.

MOTHER   I were then uncivil, madam.

LIVIA
Go to then, set your men; we'll have whole nights
Of mirth together ere we be much older, wench.

MOTHER
As good now tell her, then, for she will know't;   205
I have always found her a most friendly lady.

LIVIA
Why widow, where's your mind?

MOTHER   Troth, ev'n at home,
                                                    madam.
To tell you truth, I left a gentlewoman
Ev'n sitting all alone, which is uncomfortable,
Especially to young bloods.

LIVIA   Another excuse!   210

MOTHER
No, as I hope for health madam, that's a truth.
Please you to send and see.

LIVIA   What gentlewoman? Pish!

199 *neighbourhood* being neighbours

MOTHER
Wife to my son, indeed, but not known, madam,
To any but yourself.
LIVIA   Now I beshrew you!
Could you be so unkind to her and me,   215
To come and not bring her? 'Faith, 'tis not friendly!
MOTHER
I feared to be too bold.
LIVIA   Too bold? Oh what's become
Of the true hearty love was wont to be
'Mongst neighbours in old time!
MOTHER   And she's a stranger,
                                        madam.
LIVIA
The more should be her welcome. When is courtesy   220
In better practice, than when 'tis employed
In entertaining strangers? I could chide, i'faith.
Leave her behind, poor gentlewoman, alone too!
Make some amends, and send for her betimes; go.
MOTHER
Please you command one of your servants, madam.   225
LIVIA
Within there!

Enter SERVANT

SERVANT   Madam?
LIVIA   Attend the gentlewoman.
MOTHER
It must be carried wondrous privately
From my son's knowledge; he'll break out in storms else.
Hark you sir.   [*she gives instructions; exit* SERVANT]
LIVIA   Now comes in the heat of your part.
GUARDIANO
True, I know it, lady; and if I be out,   230
May the duke banish me from all employments,
Wanton or serious.
LIVIA   So, have you sent, widow?
MOTHER
Yes madam, he's almost at home by this.
LIVIA
And 'faith, let me entreat you, that henceforward
All such unkind faults may be swept from friendship,   235
Which does but dim the lustre. And think thus much:
It is a wrong to me, that have ability
To bid friends welcome, when you keep 'em from me;

You cannot set greater dishonour near me,
For bounty is the credit and the glory　　　　　　　　240
Of those that have enough. I see y'are sorry,
And the good 'mends is made by't.

MOTHER　　　　　　　　　　　Here she'is, madam.

Enter BIANCA, *and* SERVANT [*who shows her in, then goes off*]

BIANCA
I wonder how she comes to send for me now?

LIVIA
Gentlewoman, y'are most welcome, trust me y'are,
As courtesy can make one, or respect　　　　　　　　245
Due to the presence of you.

BIANCA　　　　　　　　　I give you thanks, lady.

LIVIA
I heard you were alone, and 't had appeared
An ill condition in me, though I knew you not,
Nor ever saw you (yet humanity
Thinks ev'ry case her own) to have kept your company　　250
Here from you and left you all solitary.
I rather ventured upon boldness then
As the least fault, and wished your presence here—
A thing most happily motioned of that gentleman,
Whom I request you, for his care and pity,　　　　　255
To honour and reward with your acquaintance;
A gentleman that ladies' rights stands for:
That's his profession.

BIANCA　　　　　　　'Tis a noble one,
And honours my acquaintance.

GUARDIANO　　　　　　　　All my intentions
Are servants to such mistresses.

BIANCA　　　　　　　　'Tis your modesty,　　　　260
It seems, that makes your deserts speak so low, sir.

LIVIA
Come widow—look you, lady, here's our business;
Are we not well employed, think you? an old quarrel
Between us, that will never be at an end.

BIANCA　　　　　　　　　　No?
And methinks there's men enough to part you, lady.　　265

LIVIA
Ho—but they set us on, let us come off
As well as we can, poor souls; men care no farther.

242 *'mends* amends
254 *motioned of* proposed by

I pray sit down, forsooth, if you have the patience
To look upon two weak and tedious gamesters.

GUARDIANO
'Faith madam, set these by till evening;   270
You'll have enough on't then. The gentlewoman,
Being a stranger, would take more delight
To see your rooms and pictures.

LIVIA   Marry, good sir,
And well remembered! I beseech you show 'em her,
That will beguile time well; pray heartily, do sir—   275
I'll do as much for you; here, take these keys,
Show her the monument too—and that's a thing
Everyone sees not; you can witness that, widow.

MOTHER
And that's worth sight indeed, madam.

BIANCA   Kind lady,
I fear I came to be a trouble to you.   280

LIVIA
Oh, nothing less, forsooth.

BIANCA
And to this courteous gentleman,
That wears a kindness in his breast so noble
And bounteous to the welcome of a stranger.

GUARDIANO
If you but give acceptance to my service,   285
You do the greatest grace and honour to me
That courtesy can merit.

BIANCA   I were too blame else,
And out of fashion much; I pray you lead, sir.

LIVIA
After a game or two we'are for you, gentlefolks.

GUARDIANO
We wish no better seconds in society   290
Than your discourses, madam, and your partner's there.

MOTHER
I thank your praise. I listened to you, sir,
Though when you spoke there came a paltry rook
Full in my way, and chokes up all my game.
                              Exit GUARDIANO *and* BIANCA

LIVIA
Alas, poor widow, I shall be too hard for thee.   295

MOTHER
Y'are cunning at the game, I'll be sworn, madam.

LIVIA
It will be found so, ere I give you over.

She that can place her man well—
MOTHER   As you do, madam—
LIVIA
As I shall wench—can never lose her game.
Nay, nay, the black king's mine.
MOTHER   Cry you mercy, madam.   300
LIVIA
And this my queen.
MOTHER   I see't now.
LIVIA   Here's a duke
Will strike a sure stroke for the game anon;
Your pawn cannot come back to relieve itself.
MOTHER
I know that, madam.
LIVIA   You play well the whilst;
How she belies her skill! I hold two ducats   305
I give you check and mate to your white king,
Simplicity itself, your saintish king there.
MOTHER
Well, ere now, lady,
I have seen the fall of subtlety. Jest on.
LIVIA
Ay, but simplicity receives two for one.   310
MOTHER
What remedy but patience!

Enter above GUARDIANO *and* BIANCA

BIANCA   Trust me, sir,
Mine eye nev'r met with fairer ornaments.

300 *Cry you mercy.* 'If you take up your Adversaries man, and after think
   best to let it stand untaken, before you set your own piece in place
   thereof, you must cry him mercy or lose the Game' (Cotton, p. 77).
301 *duke.* An alternative name for the rook; Livia's apparent identification
   at this point of the duke of Florence with the chessman is confusing:
   Bianca's seducer is the black king of line 300, and Guardiano is the rook:
   IGNATIUS
       Dukes? they're called Rooks by some.
   ERROR   Corruptively!
       Le Roc the word, *Custode de la Roche*,
       The Keeper of the Forts, in whom both Kings
       Repose much confidence
                                    (*A Game at Chess*, Induction, 55–8).
303 *pawn . . . itself.* 'a Pawn is the soonest ensnared, because he cannot go
   back for succour or relief' (Cotton, p. 67).

GUARDIANO
  Nay, livelier, I'm persuaded, neither Florence
  Nor Venice can produce.
BIANCA   Sir, my opinion
  Takes your part highly.
GUARDIANO   There's a better piece   315
  Yet than all these.   [*Enter*] DUKE *above*
BIANCA   Not possible, sir.
GUARDIANO   Believe it;
  You'll say so when you see't. Turn but your eye now,
  Y'are upon it presently.   *Exit*
BIANCA   Oh sir!
DUKE   He's gone, beauty!
  Pish, look not after him, he's but a vapour
  That when the sun appears is seen no more.   320
BIANCA
  Oh treachery to honour!
DUKE   Prithee tremble not.
  I feel thy breast shake like a turtle panting
  Under a loving hand that makes much on't.
  Why art so fearful? as I'm friend to brightness,
  There's nothing but respect and honour near thee.   325
  You know me, you have seen me; here's a heart
  Can witness I have seen thee.
BIANCA   The more's my danger.
DUKE
  The more's thy happiness. Pish, strive not, sweet!
  This strength were excellent employed in love, now,
  But here 'tis spent amiss. Strive not to seek   330
  Thy liberty and keep me still in prison.
  I'faith, you shall not out till I'm released now,
  We'll both be freed together, or stay still by't;
  So is captivity pleasant.
BIANCA   Oh my lord!
DUKE
  I am not here in vain: have but the leisure   335
  To think on that, and thou'lt be soon resolved.
  The lifting of thy voice is but like one
  That does exalt his enemy, who, proving high,
  Lays all the plots to confound him that raised him.
  Take warning, I beseech thee; thou seem'st to me   340

---

316 s.d. above. Bullen is probably correct in directing *Draws a curtain, and
    discovers the* DUKE. Guardiano and Bianca have already entered
    '*above*' (line 311), and there can hardly have been three acting levels.

A creature so composed of gentleness
And delicate meekness, such as bless the faces
Of figures that are drawn for goddesses
And make art proud to look upon her work,
I should be sorry the least force should lay   345
An unkind touch upon thee.
BIANCA   Oh my extremity!
My lord, what seek you?
DUKE   Love.
BIANCA   'Tis gone already;
I have a husband.
DUKE   That's a single comfort;
Take a friend to him.
BIANCA   That's a double mischief,
Or else there's no religion.
DUKE   Do not tremble   350
At fears of thine own making.
BIANCA   Nor, great lord,
Make me not bold with death and deeds of ruin
Because they fear not you; me they must fright,
Then am I best in health. Should thunder speak
And none regard it, it had lost the name,   355
And were as good be still. I'm not like those
That take their soundest sleeps in greatest tempests;
Then wake I most, the weather fearfullest,
And call for strength to virtue.
DUKE   Sure I think
Thou know'st the way to please me; I affect   360
A passionate pleading 'bove an easy yielding—
But never pitied any: they deserve none
That will not pity me. I can command:
Think upon that. Yet if thou truly knewest
The infinite pleasure my affection takes   365
In gentle, fair entreatings, when love's businesses
Are carried courteously 'twixt heart and heart,
You'ld make more haste to please me.
BIANCA   Why should you
                                        seek, sir,
To take away that you can never give?
DUKE
But I give better in exchange—wealth, honour.   370
She that is fortunate in a duke's favour

344 *make* ed (makes O)
353 *fear* frighten

Lights on a tree that bears all women's wishes:
If your own mother saw you pluck fruit there,
She would commend your wit, and praise the time
Of your nativity. Take hold of glory.   375
Do not I know y'have cast away your life
Upon necessities, means merely doubtful
To keep you in indifferent health and fashion
(A thing I heard too lately and soon pitied).
And can you be so much your beauty's enemy   380
To kiss away a month or two in wedlock,
And weep whole years in wants for ever after?
Come, play the wise wench, and provide for ever:
Let storms come when they list, they find thee sheltered;
Should any doubt arise, let nothing trouble thee.   385
Put trust in our love for the managing
Of all to thy heart's peace. We'll walk together,
And show a thankful joy for both our fortunes.

Exit [both] above

LIVIA
Did not I say my duke would fetch you over, widow?
MOTHER
I think you spoke in earnest when you said it, madam.   390
LIVIA
And my black king makes all the haste he can, too.
MOTHER
Well, madam, we may meet with him in time yet.
LIVIA
I have given thee blind mate twice.
MOTHER   You may see, madam,
My eyes begin to fail.
LIVIA   I'll swear they do, wench.

Enter GUARDIANO

GUARDIANO
I can but smile as often as I think on't!   395
How prettily the poor fool was beguiled,
How unexpectedly! It's a witty age;

383 *wise* ed (wife O)

372–3 *tree ... fruit.* The duke seems to be advocating Eve's action in
   plucking the apple of knowledge.
393 *blind mate.* 'that is when your Adversary gives you a check that you
   cannot avoid by any means, and is indeed a *Mate absolute*; but he not
   seeing it to be a Mate, says only to you *check*, and it is therefore called a
   Blind-Mate: this should be both loss of Game and stake if you before
   agree not to the contrary' (Cotton, p. 75).

Never were finer snares for women's honesties
Than are devised in these days; no spider's web
Made of a daintier thread, than are now practised 400
To catch love's flesh-fly by the silver wing.
Yet to prepare her stomach by degrees
To Cupid's feast, because I saw 'twas queasy,
I showed her naked pictures by the way—
A bit to stay the appetite. Well, advancement, 405
I venture hard to find thee; if thou com'st
With a greater title set upon thy crest,
I'll take that first cross patiently, and wait
Until some other comes greater than that.
I'll endure all. 410

LIVIA
The game's ev'n at the best now; you may see, widow,
How all things draw to an end.

MOTHER   Ev'n so do I, madam.

LIVIA
I pray take some of your neighbours along with you.

MOTHER
They must be those are almost twice your years, then,
If they be chose fit matches for my time, madam.

LIVIA   415
Has not my duke bestirred himself?

MOTHER   Yes, 'faith madam,
H'as done me all the mischief in this game.

LIVIA
H'as showed himself in's kind.

MOTHER   In's kind, call you it?
I may swear that.

LIVIA   Yes 'faith, and keep your oath.

GUARDIANO
Hark, list! there's somebody coming down; 'tis she. 420

Enter BIANCA

BIANCA
Now bless me from a blasting! I saw that now
Fearful for any woman's eye to look on.
Infectious mists and mildews hang at's eyes,
The weather of a doomsday dwells upon him.

407 *a greater title* i.e. pander

---

404 *naked pictures.* Part of the penance imposed on the White Queen's
Pawn by the Black House was to kneel for twelve hours 'in a room
fill'd all with Aretine's pictures' (*A Game at Chess*, II, ii, 255).

Yet since mine honour's leprous, why should I   425
Preserve that fair that caused the leprosy?
Come, poison all at once! Thou in whose baseness
The bane of virtue broods, I'm bound in soul
Eternally to curse thy smooth-browed treachery
That wore the fair veil of a friendly welcome,   430
And I a stranger; think upon't, 'tis worth it.
Murders piled up upon a guilty spirit
At his last breath will not lie heavier
Than this betraying act upon thy conscience.
Beware of off'ring the first-fruits to sin: 435
His weight is deadly who commits with strumpets
After they have been abased and made for use;
If they offend to th'death, as wise men know,
How much more they, then, that first make 'em so?
I give thee that to feed on. I'm made bold now,   440
I thank thy treachery; sin and I'm acquainted,
No couple greater; and I'm like that great one
Who, making politic use of a base villain,
'He likes the treason well, but hates the traitor';
So I hate thee, slave.

GUARDIANO   Well, so the duke love me   445
I fare not much amiss then; two great feasts
Do seldom come together in one day,
We must not look for 'em.

BIANCA   What, at it still, mother?

MOTHER
You see we sit by't; are you so soon returned?

LIVIA
So lively and so cheerful! a good sign, that.   450

MOTHER
You have not seen all since, sure?

BIANCA   That have I, mother,
The monument and all: I'm so beholding
To this kind, honest, courteous gentleman.
You'ld little think it, mother—showed me all,
Had me from place to place so fashionably;   455
The kindness of some people, how't exceeds!
'Faith, I have seen that I little thought to see
I'th'morning when I rose.

425 *why* ed (who O)   436 *commits* fornicates

---

244 *that great one*. Machiavelli. The murder of Lightborn in *Edward II*
(Act V scene v) is a good example of loving the treason and hating the
traitor.

MOTHER   Nay, so I told you
  Before you saw't, it would prove worth your sight.
  I give you great thanks for my daughter, sir,   460
  And all your kindness towards her.
GUARDIANO   Oh good widow!
  —Much good may't do her—forty weeks hence, i'faith.

                    Enter SERVANT

LIVIA
  Now sir?
SERVANT   May't please you, madam, to walk in;
  Supper's upon the table.
LIVIA   Yes, we come.
  Will't please you, gentlewoman?
BIANCA   Thanks, virtuous lady   465
  —Y'are a damned bawd! I'll follow you, forsooth;
  Pray take my mother in—an old ass go with you—
  This gentleman and I vow not to part.
LIVIA
  Then get you both before.
BIANCA   There lies his art.
                    Exeunt [BIANCA *and* GUARDIANO]

LIVIA
  Widow, I'll follow you.   [*Exit* MOTHER]

                    Is't so, 'damned bawd'!   470
  Are you so bitter? 'Tis but want of use;
  Her tender modesty is sea-sick a little,
  Being not accustomed to the breaking billow
  Of woman's wavering faith, blown with temptations.
  'Tis but a qualm of honour, 'twill away;   475
  A little bitter for the time, but lasts not.
  Sin tastes at the first draught like wormwood water,
  But drunk again, 'tis nectar ever after.   *Exit*

                    Act III, Scene i

                    Enter MOTHER

MOTHER
  I would my son would either keep at home

462 *may't* ed (may O)

---

472 *sea-sick*. '. . . yet indeed 'tis the fashion of any courtesan to be sea-sick
  i'th'first voyage' (*Michaelmas Term*, I, ii, 10).

Or I were in my grave!
She was but one day abroad, but ever since
She's grown so cutted, there's no speaking to her.
Whether the sight of great cheer at my lady's,   5
And such mean fare at home, work discontent in her,
I know not; but I'm sure she's strangely altered.
I'll nev'r keep daughter-in-law i'th'house with me
Again, if I had an hundred. When read I of any
That agreed long together, but she and her mother   10
Fell out in the first quarter—nay, sometime
A grudging of a scolding the first week, by'r Lady.
So takes the new disease, methinks, in my house.
I'm weary of my part, there's nothing likes her;
I know not how to please her here o' late.   15
And here she comes.

Enter BIANCA

BIANCA   This is the strangest house
For all defects, as ever gentlewoman
Made shift withal, to pass away her love in!
Why is there not a cushion-cloth of drawn work,
Or some fair cut-work pinned up in my bed-chamber,   20
A silver-and-gilt casting-bottle hung by't?
Nay, since I am content to be so kind to you,
To spare you for a silver basin and ewer,
Which one of my fashion looks for of duty
She's never offered under, where she sleeps.   25
MOTHER
She talks of things here my whole state's not worth.
BIANCA
Never a green silk quilt is there i'th'house, mother,
To cast upon my bed?
MOTHER   No by troth is there,
Nor orange-tawny neither.

4 *cutted* querulous
20 *cut-work* lace   21 *casting-bottle* bottle for sprinkling scent

---

13 *the new disease.* Its symptoms are described by Jonson:
    A new disease? I know not, new, or old,
    But it may well be called poor mortals' plague:
    For, like a pestilence, it doth infect
    The houses of the brain. First, it begins
    Solely to work upon the fantasy,
    Filling her seat with such pestiferous air,
    As soon corrupts the judgement . . .
                              (*Every Man In His Humour*, II, i, 219–24).

BIANCA   Here's a house
For a young gentlewoman to be got with child in!   30
MOTHER
Yes, simple though you make it, there has been three
Got in a year in't—since you move me to't—
And all as sweet-faced children and as lovely
As you'll be mother of: I will not spare you.
What, cannot children be begot, think you,   35
Without gilt casting-bottles? Yes, and as sweet ones:
The miller's daughter brings forth as white boys
As she that bathes herself with milk and bean-flour.
'Tis an old saying 'one may keep good cheer
In a mean house': so may true love affect   40
After the rate of princes, in a cottage.
BIANCA
Troth, you speak wondrous well for your old house here;
'Twill shortly fall down at your feet to thank you,
Or stoop when you go to bed, like a good child,
To ask you blessing. Must I live in want,   45
Because my fortune matched me with your son?
Wives do not give away themselves to husbands
To the end to be quite cast away; they look
To be the better used and tendered rather,
Highlier respected, and maintained the richer;   50
They're well rewarded else for the free gift
Of their whole life to a husband. I ask less now
Than what I had at home when I was a maid
And at my father's house; kept short of that
Which a wife knows she must have—nay, and will   55
—Will, mother, if she be not a fool born—
And report went of me that I could wrangle
For what I wanted when I was two hours old;
And by that copy, this land still I hold.
You hear me, mother.   *Exit*

37 *white boys* darlings   59 *copy* copyhold (legal)

---

38 *bathes ... milk.* The epitome of wasteful luxury: the proud woman
   'grieve[s] her maker In sinful baths of milk, when many an infant
   starves' (Tourneur, *The Revenger's Tragedy*, III, v, 84–5).
38 *bean-flour.*
       I should be tumbling in cold baths now,
       Under each armpit a fine bean-flour bag,
       To screw out whiteness when I list
                    (Middleton *et al.*, *The Old Law*, II, ii, 11–13).
39–40 *one ... house.* The proverb has many variants: 'Content lodges
   oftener in cottages than palaces' (Tilley, C 626).

MOTHER   Ay, too plain, methinks;   60
  And were I somewhat deafer when you spake
  'Twere nev'r a whit the worse for my quietness.
  'Tis the most sudden'st, strangest alteration,
  And the most subtlest that ev'r wit at threescore
  Was puzzled to find out. I know no cause for't; but   65
  She's no more like the gentlewoman at first
  Than I am like her that nev'r lay with man yet,
  And she's a very young thing where'er she be.
  When she first lighted here, I told her then
  How mean she should find all things; she was pleased,
      forsooth,   70
  None better: I laid open all defects to her;
  She was contented still. But the devil's in her,
  Nothing contents her now. Tonight my son
  Promised to be at home; would he were come once,
  For I'm weary of my charge, and life too.   75
  She'ld be served all in silver, by her good will,
  By night and day; she hates the name of pewter
  More than sick men the noise, or diseased bones
  That quake at fall o'th'hammer, seeming to have
  A fellow-feeling with't at every blow.   80
  What course shall I think on? she frets me so.
                    [*Withdraws to back of stage*]

                    Enter LEANTIO

LEANTIO
  How near am I now to a happiness
  That earth exceeds not—not another like it!
  The treasures of the deep are not so precious
  As are the concealed comforts of a man,   85
  Locked up in woman's love. I scent the air
  Of blessings when I come but near the house.
  What a delicious breath marriage sends forth;
  The violet-bed's not sweeter. Honest wedlock
  Is like a banqueting-house built in a garden,   90

---

74 *once* once for all   77 *pewter* ed (pewterer O)

---

78 *the noise.* 'Sounds supposed to have been heard before the death of any
   person' (*English Dialect Dictionary*).
90 *banqueting-house . . . garden.* Bacon's model garden was to be graced
   with such a banqueting-house: 'I wish also, in the very middle, a fair
   mount . . . and the whole mount to be thirty foot high; and some fine
   banqueting-house, with chimneys neatly cast, and without too much
   glass' (Essay 'Of Gardens').

On which the spring's chaste flowers take delight
To cast their modest odours—when base lust,
With all her powders, paintings and best pride,
Is but a fair house built by a ditch side.
When I behold a glorious dangerous strumpet,   95
Sparkling in beauty and destruction too,
Both at a twinkling, I do liken straight
Her beautified body to a goodly temple
That's built on vaults where carcasses lie rotting:
And so by little and little I shrink back again,   100
And quench desire with a cool meditation;
And I'm as well, methinks. Now for a welcome
Able to draw men's envies upon man:
A kiss now that will hang upon my lip
As sweet as morning dew upon a rose,   105
And full as long. After a five days' fast
She'll be so greedy now, and cling about me,
I take care how I shall be rid of her;
And here't begins.

                    [*Enter* BIANCA; MOTHER *comes forward*]

BIANCA   Oh sir, y'are welcome home.
MOTHER
  Oh is he come? I am glad on't.
LEANTIO   Is that all?   110
  Why this? as dreadful now as sudden death
  To some rich man that flatters all his sins
  With promise of repentance when he's old,
  And dies in the midway before he comes to't.
  Sure y'are not well Bianca! How dost, prithee?   115
BIANCA
  I have been better than I am at this time.
LEANTIO
  Alas, I thought so.
BIANCA   Nay, I have been worse too
  Than now you see me sir.
LEANTIO   I'm glad thou mend'st yet;
  I feel my heart mend too. How came it to thee?
  Has anything disliked thee in my absence?   120

98-9 *goodly . . . rotting.* 'Woe unto you, scribes and Pharisees, hypocrites!
  for ye are like unto whited sepulchres, which indeed appear beautiful
  outward, but are within full of dead men's bones, and of all uncleanness'
  (*St Matthew*, xxiii, 27).

BIANCA

  No, certain; I have had the best content
  That Florence can afford.

LEANTIO   Thou makest the best on't;
  Speak mother, what's the cause? you must needs know.

MOTHER

  Troth, I know none, son; let her speak herself.
  —Unless it be the same gave Lucifer   125
  A tumbling-cast, that's pride.

BIANCA

  Methinks this house stands nothing to my mind,
  I'ld have some pleasant lodging i'th'high street, sir;
  Or if 'twere near the court, sir, that were much better—
  'Tis a sweet recreation for a gentlewoman   130
  To stand in a bay-window and see gallants.

LEANTIO

  Now I have another temper, a mere stranger
  To that of yours, it seems; I should delight
  To see none but yourself.

BIANCA   I praise not that:
  Too fond is as unseemly as too churlish.   135
  I would not have a husband of that proneness
  To kiss me before company, for a world!
  Beside, 'tis tedious to see one thing still, sir,
  Be it the best that ever heart affected—
  Nay, were't yourself, whose love had power, you know, 140
  To bring me from my friends, I would not stand thus
  And gaze upon you always; troth, I could not, sir.
  As good be blind and have no use of sight
  As look on one thing still: what's the eye's treasure
  But change of objects? You are learned, sir,   145
  And know I speak not ill. 'Tis full as virtuous

---

126 *tumbling-cast* wrestling throw   146 *'Tis* ed ('till O)

128–31 *I'ld . . . gallants.* 'the poore wife [has not] liberty to looke out of the
    windowe, especially if it be towards the streete' (Moryson 4, p. 151).
    Bianca is virtually proclaiming herself a whore—offering herself in the
    window:
        I'll have that window next the street dammed up;
        It gives too full a prospect to temptation,
        And courts a gazer's glances. There's a lust
        Committed by the eye, that sweats and travails,
        Plots, wakes, contrives, till the deformed bear-whelp
        Adultery be licked into the act
                     (Ford, *The Broken Heart*, II, i, 1–6).

For woman's eye to look on several men,
As for her heart, sir, to be fixed on one.

LEANTIO
Now thou com'st home to me; a kiss for that word.

BIANCA
No matter for a kiss, sir; let it pass;   150
'Tis but a toy, we'll not so much as mind it.
Let's talk of other business and forget it.
What news now of the pirates; any stirring?
Prithee discourse a little.

MOTHER   I am glad he's here yet
To see her tricks himself; I had lied monstrously   155
If I had told 'em first.

LEANTIO   Speak, what's the humour, sweet,
You make your lip so strange? this was not wont.

BIANCA
Is there no kindness betwixt man and wife
Unless they make a pigeon-house of friendship
And be still billing? 'tis the idlest fondness   160
That ever was invented, and 'tis pity
It's grown a fashion for poor gentlewomen;
There's many a disease kissed in a year by't,
And a French curtsy made to't. Alas, sir,
Think of the world, how we shall live, grow serious;   165
We have been married a whole fortnight now.

LEANTIO
How? a whole fortnight! why, is that so long?

BIANCA
'Tis time to leave off dalliance; 'tis a doctrine
Of your own teaching, if you be remembered,
And I was bound to obey it.

MOTHER   Here's one fits him!   170
This was well catched, i'faith son—like a fellow
That rids another country of a plague
And brings it home with him to his own house.
Who knocks?   *Knock within*

LEANTIO   Who's there now? Withdraw you, Bianca;
Thou art a gem no stranger's eye must see,   175
Howev'r thou please now to look dull on me.

                              Exit [BIANCA]

176 *thou please* ed (thou pleas'd O; thou'rt pleas'd Bullen)

---

153 *news . . . pirates.* The duke of Florence kept a watch on the coasts 'for
    feare of African pyrates, whome the Duke yearely provoked by the
    Gallyes he sett out to spoyle the Turkes' (Moryson 4, p. 146).
164 *French curtsy.* An oblique reference to syphilis, the 'French disease'.

Enter MESSENGER

Y'are welcome sir; to whom your business, pray?

MESSENGER
To one I see not here now.

LEANTIO   Who should that be, sir?

MESSENGER
A young gentlewoman I was sent to.

LEANTIO
A young gentlewoman?

MESSENGER   Ay sir, about sixteen.   180
Why look you wildly sir?

LEANTIO   At your strange error;
Y'have mistook the house, sir, there's none such here,
I assure you.

MESSENGER   I assure you too:
The man that sent me cannot be mistook.

LEANTIO
Why, who is't sent you, sir?

MESSENGER   The duke.

LEANTIO   The duke!   185

MESSENGER
Yes, he entreats her company at a banquet
At Lady Livia's house.

LEANTIO   Troth, shall I tell you, sir,
It is the most erroneous business
That ere your honest pains was abused with.
I pray forgive me if I smile a little—   190
I cannot choose, i'faith sir, at an error
So comical as this (I mean no harm, though).
His grace has been most wondrous ill informed;
Pray so return it, sir. What should her name be?

MESSENGER
That I shall tell you straight too: Bianca Capello.   195

LEANTIO
How sir, Bianca? what do you call th'other?

MESSENGER
Capello. Sir, it seems you know no such, then?

LEANTIO
Who should this be? I never heard o'th'name.

MESSENGER
Then 'tis a sure mistake.

LEANTIO   What if you enquired
In the next street, sir? I saw gallants there   200

In the new houses that are built of late.
Ten to one, there you find her.
MESSENGER   Nay, no matter,
I will return the mistake and seek no further.
LEANTIO
Use your own will and pleasure sir; y'are welcome.
                                        Exit MESSENGER
What shall I think of first? Come forth Bianca.   205
Thou art betrayed, I fear me.
                    [*Enter* BIANCA]
BIANCA   Betrayed—how sir?
LEANTIO
The duke knows thee.
BIANCA   Knows me! how know you that, sir?
LEANTIO
Has got thy name.
BIANCA   Ay, and my good name too,
That's worse o'th'twain.
LEANTIO   How comes this work about?
BIANCA
How should the duke know me? can you guess, mother?   210
MOTHER
Not I with all my wits; sure, we kept house close.
LEANTIO
Kept close! not all the locks in Italy
Can keep you women so. You have been gadding,
And ventured out at twilight to th'court-green yonder,
And met the gallant bowlers coming home,   215
Without your masks too, both of you; I'll be hanged else!
Thou hast been seen, Bianca, by some stranger;
Never excuse it.
BIANCA   I'll not seek the way, sir.
Do you think y'have married me to mew me up
Not to be seen; what would you make of me?   220
LEANTIO
A good wife, nothing else.
BIANCA   Why, so are some
That are seen ev'ry day, else the devil take 'em.
LEANTIO
No more then: I believe all virtuous in thee

213 *gadding.* 'A dishonest woman is hardly kept within her owne house, but
    shee must be a ramping and aroysting about to make herself knowne'
    (Barnaby Rich, *The Excellencie of Good Women* (1613), p. 24).
216 *Without your masks.* Young Italian wives were 'covered with vayles
    when they go abroad' (Moryson 4, p. 409).

Without an argument. 'Twas but thy hard chance
To be seen somewhere; there lies all the mischief,   225
But I have devised a riddance.

MOTHER   Now I can tell you, son,
The time and place.

LEANTIO   When? where?

MOTHER   What wits have I!
When you last took your leave, if you remember,
You left us both at window.

LEANTIO   Right, I know that.

MOTHER
And not the third part of an hour after   230
The duke passed by in a great solemnity
To St Mark's temple; and to my apprehension
He looked up twice to th'window.

LEANTIO   Oh, there quickened
The mischief of this hour.

BIANCA   If you call't mischief,
It is a thing I fear I am conceived with.   235

LEANTIO
Looked he up twice, and could you take no warning!

MOTHER
Why, once may do as much harm, son, as a thousand:
Do not you know one spark has fired an house
As well as a whole furnace?

LEANTIO   My heart flames for't!
Yet let's be wise and keep all smothered closely;   240
I have bethought a means. Is the door fast?

MOTHER
I locked it myself after him.

LEANTIO   You know, mother,
At the end of the dark parlour there's a place
So artificially contrived for a conveyance
No search could ever find it—when my father   245
Kept in for manslaughter, it was his sanctuary:
There will I lock my life's best treasure up.
Bianca!

BIANCA   Would you keep me closer yet?
Have you the conscience? Y'are best ev'n choke me up, sir!
You make me fearful of your health and wits,   250
You cleave to such wild courses. What's the matter?

LEANTIO
Why, are you so insensible of your danger

244 *artificially* artfully   244 *conveyance* secret passage (O.E.D. 12a)

To ask that now? The duke himself has sent for you
To Lady Livia's, to a banquet forsooth.

BIANCA
Now I beshrew you heartily. Has he so! 255
And you the man would never yet vouchsafe
To tell me on't till now! you show your loyalty
And honesty at once; and so farewell, sir.

LEANTIO
Bianca, whither now?

BIANCA   Why, to the duke, sir.
You say he sent for me. 260

LEANTIO   But thou dost not mean
To go, I hope.

BIANCA   No? I shall prove unmannerly,
Rude and uncivil, mad, and imitate you?
Come, mother, come; follow his humour no longer.
We shall be all executed for treason shortly.

MOTHER
Not I, i'faith; I'll first obey the duke, 265
And taste of a good banquet; I'm of thy mind.
I'll step but up and fetch two handkerchiefs
To pocket up some sweetmeats, and o'ertake thee. *Exit*

BIANCA
Why, here's an old wench would trot into a bawd now
For some dry sucket or a colt in marchpane. *Exit* 270

LEANTIO
Oh thou the ripe time of man's misery, wedlock,
When all his thoughts, like over-laden trees,

267–8 *handkerchiefs ... sweetmeats.* 'I come not empty-pocketed from a
banquet, I learn'd that of my haberdasher's wife' (*The Witch*, I, ii, 217–8).
270 *dry ... marchpane.* Gervase Markham gives instructions to the house-
wife about the kind and order of dishes to be served at a banquet:
  ... when they goe to the table, you shall first send forth a dish made
  for shew onely, as Beast, bird, Fish, or Fowl, according to invention:
  then your Marchpane, then preserved Fruite, then a Paste, then a
  wet Sucket, then a dry Sucket, Marmelade, Cumfetts, Apples, Pears,
  Wardens, Oranges and Lemmons sliced; and then Wafers, and another
  dish of preserved Fruites, and so consequently all the rest before
                              (*Country Contentments* (1623), p. 125).
Sucket (wet and dry) was a kind of crystallised fruit. *Marchpane*
(= marzipan) could be moulded into the forms of bulls, rams, horses,
etc.: '*The banquet is brought in, six of* WEATHERWISE'S *Tenants carrying
the Twelve Signs ... made of banqueting stuff*' (Middleton, *No Wit/
Help Like a Woman's*, II, i, 96 s.d.).

Crack with the fruits they bear, in cares, in jealousies—
Oh that's a fruit that ripens hastily
After 'tis knit to marriage: it begins   275
As soon as the sun shines upon the bride
A little to show colour. Blessed powers!
Whence comes this alteration? the distractions,
The fears and doubts it brings are numberless;
And yet the cause I know not. What a peace   280
Has he that never marries! if he knew
The benefit he enjoyed, or had the fortune
To come and speak with me, he should know then
The infinite wealth he had, and discern rightly
The greatness of his treasure by my loss.   285
Nay, what a quietness has he 'bove mine,
That wears his youth out in a strumpet's arms,
And never spends more care upon a woman
Than at the time of lust; but walks away,
And if he finds her dead at his return,   290
His pity is soon done: he breaks a sigh
In many parts, and gives her but a piece on't.
But all the fears, shames, jealousies, costs and troubles,
And still renewed cares of a marriage bed
Live in the issue when the wife is dead.   295

Enter MESSENGER

MESSENGER
    A good perfection to your thoughts.
LEANTIO   The news, sir?
MESSENGER
    Though you were pleased of late to pin an error on me,
    You must not shift another in your stead too:
    The duke has sent me for you.
LEANTIO   How, for me, sir?
    I see then 'tis my theft; w'are both betrayed.   300
    Well, I'm not the first has stol'n away a maid:
    My countrymen have used it. I'll along with you, sir.
                                                            Exeunt

Act III, Scene ii
A banquet prepared:

Enter GUARDIANO *and* WARD

GUARDIANO
    Take you especial note of such a gentlewoman,
    She's here on purpose; I have invited her,
    Her father and her uncle, to this banquet.

Mark her behaviour well, it does concern you;
And what her good parts are, as far as time   5
And place can modestly require a knowledge of,
Shall be laid open to your understanding.
You know I'm both your guardian and your uncle:
My care of you is double, ward and nephew,
And I'll express it here.
WARD   'Faith, I should know her   10
Now, by her mark, among a thousand women:
A little, pretty, deft and tidy thing, you say?
GUARDIANO
Right.
WARD
With a lusty sprouting sprig in her hair?
GUARDIANO
Thou goest the right way still; take one mark more: 15
Thou shalt nev'r find her hand out of her uncle's,
Or else his out of hers, if she be near him:
The love of kindred never yet stuck closer
Than their's to one another; he that weds her
Marries her uncle's heart too.   *Cornets*
WARD   Say you so, sir;   20
Then I'll be asked i'th'church to both of 'em.
GUARDIANO
Fall back, here comes the duke.
WARD
He brings a gentlewoman,
I should fall forward rather.

Enter DUKE, BIANCA, FABRITIO, HIPPOLITO, LIVIA, MOTHER,
          ISABELLA, *and Attendants*

DUKE
Come Bianca,   25
Of purpose sent into the world to show
Perfection once in woman; I'll believe
Henceforward they have ev'ry one a soul too,
14 *sprig* See note at II, ii, 84
_____

28 *ev'ry one a soul.* God breathed 'the breath of life' into Adam's nostrils, 'and
   man became a living soul' (*Genesis* ii, 7) but He did not do the same for Eve:
        Man to God's image, *Eve*, to mans was made,
        Nor finde wee that God breath'd a soul in her
                              (Donne, 'To the Countess of Huntingdon').
   By this time, however, a serious medieval debate had degenerated to
   just one more insult for the exasperated male to throw at women; and
   Donne can also write 'so we have given *women* soules onely to make
   them capable of damnation?' (*Paradoxes and Problemes*, Problem 6).

'Gainst all the uncourteous opinions
That man's uncivil rudeness ever held of 'em.   30
Glory of Florence, light into mine arms!

Enter LEANTIO

BIANCA
Yon comes a grudging man will chide you, sir.
The storm is now in's heart, and would get nearer
And fall here if it durst; it pours down yonder.

DUKE
If that be he, the weather shall soon clear;   35
List and I'll tell thee how. [*Whispers to* BIANCA]

LEANTIO   A kissing too?
I see 'tis plain lust now, adultery boldened.
What will it prove anon, when 'tis stuffed full
Of wine and sweetmeats, being so impudent fasting?

DUKE
We have heard of your good parts, sir, which we honour   40
With our embrace and love. Is not the captainship
Of Rouens' citadel, since the late deceased,
Supplied by any yet?

GENTLEMAN   By none, my lord.

DUKE
Take it, the place is yours then;   [LEANTIO *kneels*]
and as faithfulness
And desert grows, our favour shall grow with't: 45
Rise now the captain of our fort at Rouens.

LEANTIO
The service of whole life give your grace thanks.

DUKE
Come, sit Bianca.

LEANTIO   This is some good yet,
And more than ev'r I looked for—a fine bit
To stay a cuckold's stomach! All preferment   50
That springs from sin and lust, it shoots up quickly,
As gardeners' crops do in the rotten'st grounds:

---

42 *Rouens*. The appointment is fictitious; and I can find no reason why
Middleton should have seized on the name Rouens (Rouans O).
50–56 *All . . . mad*. Leantio, like Bosola in Webster's *The Duchess of Malfi*,
takes on something of the traditional quality of the malcontent:
what's my place?
The provisorship o'the'horse? say then my corruption
Grew out of horse dung

(*The Duchess of Malfi*, I, ii, 206–7).

So is all means raised from base prostitution
Ev'n like a sallet growing upon a dunghill.
I'm like a thing that never was yet heard of,   55
Half merry and half mad—much like a fellow
That eats his meat with a good appetite,
And wears a plague-sore that would fright a country;
Or rather like the barren hardened ass,
That feeds on thistles till he bleeds again.   60
And such is the condition of my misery.

LIVIA
Is that your son, widow?

MOTHER   Yes, did your ladyship
Never know that till now?

LIVIA   No, trust me, did I.
—Nor ever truly felt the power of love
And pity to a man, till now I knew him.   65
I have enough to buy me my desires,
And yet to spare, that's one good comfort. Hark you?
Pray let me speak with you, sir, before you go.

LEANTIO
With me, lady? you shall; I am at your service.
—What will she say now, trow? more goodness yet?   70

WARD
I see her now, I'm sure; the ape's so little, I shall scarce
feel her! I have seen almost as tall as she sold in the fair
for tenpence. See how she simpers it—as if marmalade
would not melt in her mouth! She might have the kindness,
i'faith, to send me a gilded bull from her own trencher,   75
a ram, a goat, or somewhat to be nibbling; these women,
when they come to sweet things once, they forget all their
friends, they grow so greedy—nay, oftentimes their
husbands.

DUKE
Here's a health now, gallants,   80
To the best beauty at this day in Florence.

BIANCA
Whoe'er she be, she shall not go unpledged, sir.

---

54 *sallet* salad
59 *barren* stupid
71–9 *I see . . . husbands* (as verse O)
75 *gilded bull* See note at III, i, 270

73–4 *marmalade . . . mouth.* Proverbial: 'He looks as if butter would not
    melt in his mouth' (Tilley, B 774).

DUKE

  Nay, you're excused for this.

BIANCA   Who, I my lord?

DUKE

  Yes, by the law of Bacchus; plead your benefit:

  You are not bound to pledge your own health, lady.   85

BIANCA

  That's a good way, my lord, to keep me dry.

DUKE

  Nay then, I will not offend Venus so much;

  Let Bacchus seek his 'mends in another court.

  Here's to thyself, Bianca.

BIANCA   Nothing comes

  More welcome to that name than your grace.

LEANTIO   So, so!   90

  Here stands the poor thief now that stole the treasure,

  And he's not thought on. Ours is near kin now

  To a twin misery born into the world:

  First the hard-conscienced worldling—he hoards wealth up:

  Then comes the next, and he feasts all upon't;   95

  One's damned for getting, th'other for spending on't.

  Oh equal justice, thou hast met my sin

  With a full weight; I'm rightly now oppressed:

  All her friends' heavy hearts lie in my breast.

DUKE

  Methinks there is no spirit amongst us, gallants,   100

  But what divinely sparkles from the eyes

  Of bright Bianca; we sat all in darkness

  But for that splendour. Who was't told us lately

  Of a match-making rite, a marriage-tender?

GUARDIANO

  'Twas I, my lord.

DUKE   'Twas you indeed. Where is she?   105

GUARDIANO

  This is the gentlewoman.

FABRITIO   My lord, my daughter.

DUKE

  Why, here's some stirring yet.

FABRITIO   She's a dear child to me.

DUKE

  That must needs be, you say she is your daughter.

FABRITIO

  Nay my good lord, dear to my purse, I mean,

---

  84 *plead your benefit* claim exemption from the law

Beside my person; I nev'r reckoned that.   110
She has the full qualities of a gentlewoman;
I have brought her up to music, dancing, what not,
That may commend her sex and stir her husband.

DUKE
And which is he now?

GUARDIANO   This young heir, my lord.

DUKE
What is he brought up to?

HIPPOLITO   To cat and trap.   115

GUARDIANO
My lord, he's a great ward, wealthy but simple;
His parts consist in acres.

DUKE   Oh, wise-acres!

GUARDIANO
Y'have spoke him in a word, sir.

BIANCA   'Las, poor gentlewoman,
She's ill bestead, unless sh'as dealt the wiselier
And laid in more provision for her youth: 120
Fools will not keep in summer.

LEANTIO   No, nor such wives
From whores in winter.

DUKE   Yea, the voice too, sir?

FABRITIO
Ay, and a sweet breast too, my lord, I hope,
Or I have cast away my money wisely;
She took her pricksong earlier, my lord,   125
Than any of her kindred ever did.
A rare child, though I say't—but I'ld not have
The baggage hear so much; 'twould make her swell straight,
And maids of all things must not be puffed up.

DUKE
Let's turn us to a better banquet, then;   130
For music bids the soul of man to a feast,
And that's indeed a noble entertainment

121 *Fools . . . summer* See note at I, ii, 117
131 *of man* ed (of a man O)

---

123 *breast.* Voice: 'the fool has an excellent breast' (*Twelfth Night*, II, iii, 19).
But from Bianca's comment at lines 159–62, it would seem that the
expression is old-fashioned.

125 *pricksong.* Written vocal music; the notes were 'pricked' on to the paper.
The term allows unlimited punning: '. . . your ladyship was the first
that brought up prick-song, being nothing else but the fatal notes of
your pitiful ravishment' (the ant to the nightingale in *Father Hubburd's
Tales*, viii, 88).

Worthy Bianca's self. You shall perceive, beauty,
Our Florentine damsels are not brought up idlely.

BIANCA

They'are wiser of themselves, it seems, my lord,   135
And can take gifts, when goodness offers 'em.   *Music*

LEANTIO

True; and damnation has taught you that wisdom,
You can take gifts too. Oh that music mocks me!

LIVIA

I am as dumb to any language now
But love's, as one that never learned to speak!   140
I am not yet so old, but he may think of me.
My own fault—I have been idle a long time;
But I'll begin the week and paint tomorrow,
So follow my true labour day by day:
I never thrived so well as when I used it.   145

ISABELLA

Song

What harder chance can fall to woman,
Who was born to cleave to some man,
Than to bestow her time, youth, beauty,
Life's observance, honour, duty,
On a thing for no use good,   150
But to make physic work, or blood
Force fresh in an old lady's cheek?
She that would be
Mother of fools, let her compound with me.

WARD

Here's a tune indeed! Pish! I had rather hear one ballad   155
sung i'th'nose now, of the lamentable drowning of fat
sheep and oxen, than all these simpering tunes played upon
cats-guts and sung by little kitlings.

---

143 *paint*. Middleton shared the Jacobean loathing of cosmetics:
          I'm a woman;
     Yet, I praise heaven, I never had th'ambition
     To go about to mend a better workman:
     She ever shames herself i'th'end that does it
                    (Middleton, *The Widow*, II, i, 11–14).

146–58 Song . . . *kitlings*. O prints Isabella's song and the Ward's speech
     side by side, presumably to indicate that these take place simultaneously
     (and that the Ward does not hear the coarse insults).

151 *physic*. Laxative—which a gentle exercise would make more efficacious.

155–7 *ballad . . . oxen*. The Ward refers to the common material of the
     street ballad, the Jacobean newspaper (cf. *The Winter's Tale*, IV, iv,
     261–85).

FABRITIO
　How like you her breast now, my lord?
BIANCA　　　　　　　　　　　　　Her breast!
　He talks as if his daughter had given suck　　　　160
　Before she were married, as her betters have;
　The next he praises sure will be her nipples.
DUKE
　Methinks now, such a voice to such a husband
　Is like a jewel of unvalued worth
　Hung at a fool's ear.
FABRITIO　　　　　　　May it please your grace　　165
　To give her leave to show another quality?
DUKE
　Marry, as many good ones as you will, sir,
　The more the better welcome.
LEANTIO　　　　　　　　　　But the less
　The better practised. That soul's black indeed
　That cannot commend virtue. But who keeps it?　　170
　The extortioner will say to a sick beggar
　'Heaven comfort thee', though he give none himself.
　This good is common.
FABRITIO　　　　　　　Will it please you now, sir,
　To entreat your ward to take her by the hand
　And lead her in a dance before the duke?　　　　175
GUARDIANO
　That will I, sir; 'tis needful. Hark you, nephew.
FABRITIO
　Nay you shall see, young heir, what y'have for your money,
　Without fraud or imposture.
WARD　　　　　　　　　Dance with her!
　Not I, sweet guardiner, do not urge my heart to't,
　'Tis clean against my blood; dance with a stranger!　　180
　Let whos' will do't, I'll not begin first with her.
HIPPOLITO
　No, fear't not, fool; sh'as took a better order.
GUARDIANO
　Why, who shall take her, then?
WARD　　　　　　　　　　Some other gentleman—

175–229 Middleton no doubt knew the mystical significance which the
　　　Elizabethans attached to dancing:
　　　　　by the joyning of a man and a woman in daunsynge may be signified
　　　　　matrimonye . . . In every daunse of a moste auncient custome, there
　　　　　daunseth to gyther a man and a woman, holdyng ech other by the
　　　　　hande or the arme, whych betokeneth concorde
　　　　　　　　(Thomas Elyot, *The Boke named the Governour* (1534), p. 78).

Look, there's her uncle, a fine-timbered reveller;
Perhaps he knows the manner of her dancing too;   185
I'll have him do't before me. I have sworn, guardiner;
Then may I learn the better.

GUARDIANO   Thou'lt be an ass still.

WARD
Ay, all that 'uncle' shall not fool me out:
Pish, I stick closer to myself than so.

GUARDIANO
I must entreat you, sir, to take your niece   190
And dance with her; my ward's a little wilful,
He would have you show him the way.

HIPPOLITO   Me sir?
He shall command it at all hours; pray tell him so.

GUARDIANO
I thank you for him; he has not wit himself, sir.

HIPPOLITO
Come, my life's peace, I have a strange office on't here!   195
'Tis some man's luck to keep the joys he likes
Concealed for his own bosom; but my fortune
To set 'em out now for another's liking:
Like the mad misery of necessitous man,
That parts from his good horse with many praises,   200
And goes on foot himself. Need must be obeyed
In ev'ry action, it mars man and maid.

Music. A dance, making honours to the DUKE *and curtsy to*
themselves, both before and after

DUKE
Signor Fabritio, y'are a happy father;
Your cares and pains are fortunate; you see
Your cost bears noble fruits. Hippolito, thanks.   205

FABRITIO
Here's some amends for all my charges yet;
She wins both prick and praise where'er she comes.

DUKE
How lik'st, Bianca?

BIANCA   All things well, my lord,
But this poor gentlewoman's fortune, that's the worst.

---

184 *fine-timbered* well-built

---

207 *prick and praise*. The *prick* is the mark in the centre of an archery butt:
    '. . . are you so ignorant in the rules of courtship, to think any one
    man to bear all the prick and praise?' (Middleton, *The Family of Love*,
    II, iv, 6–8).

DUKE

There is no doubt, Bianca, she'll find leisure　　　　210
To make that good enough; he's rich and simple.

BIANCA

She has the better hope o'th'upper hand, indeed,
Which women strive for most.

GUARDIANO　　　　　　　　Do't when I bid you, sir.

WARD

I'll venture but a hornpipe with her, guardiner,
Or some such married man's dance.

GUARDIANO　　　　　　　　　　Well, venture
　　　　　　　　　　　　　　　　　　something, sir.　215

WARD

I have rhyme for what I do.

GUARDIANO　　　　　　　　But little reason, I think.

WARD

Plain men dance the measures, the cinquepace the gay;
Cuckolds dance the hornpipe, and farmers dance the hay;
Your soldiers dance the round, and maidens that grow big
Your drunkards, the canaries; your whore and bawd, the jig.　220
Here's your eight kind of dancers—he that finds the ninth,
Let him pay the minstrels.

DUKE

Oh, here he appears once in his own person!
I thought he would have married her by attorney,
And lain with her so too.

BIANCA　　　　　　　　Nay, my kind lord,　　　225
There's very seldom any found so foolish
To give away his part there.

LEANTIO　　　　　　　　Bitter scoff!
Yet I must do't. With what a cruel pride
The glory of her sin strikes by my afflictions!

Music. WARD *and* ISABELLA *dance; he ridiculously imitates*
HIPPOLITO

DUKE

This thing will make shift, sirs, to make a husband,　　　230
For aught I see in him; how think'st, Bianca?

215 *Well* ed (We'll O)
217 *measures* a stately dance
217 *cinquepace* galliard (lively, French dance)
218 *hay* a rustic dance
219 *round* the watch kept by soldiers, also circling dance
220 *Your . . . your . . .* ed (you . . . you . . . O)
220 *canaries* a quick dance (thought to come from the Canary Islands)

BIANCA
  'Faith, an ill-favoured shift, my lord. Methinks
  If he would take some voyage when he's married,
  Dangerous or long enough, and scarce be seen
  Once in nine year together, a wife then   235
  Might make indifferent shift to be content with him.

DUKE
  A kiss! that wit deserves to be made much on.
  Come, our caroche!

GUARDIANO   Stands ready for your grace.

DUKE
  My thanks to all your loves. Come, fair Bianca;
  We have took special care of you, and provided   240
  Your lodging near us now.

BIANCA   Your love is great, my lord.

DUKE
  Once more, our thanks to all.

OMNES   All blest honours guard you.

        Exeunt all but LEANTIO *and* LIVIA
          Cornets flourish

LEANTIO
  Oh, hast thou left me then, Bianca, utterly!
  Bianca! now I miss thee—Oh return,
  And save the faith of woman. I nev'r felt   245
  The loss of thee till now; 'tis an affliction
  Of greater weight than youth was made to bear—
  As if a punishment of after-life
  Were fallen upon man here, so new it is
  To flesh and blood; so strange, so insupportable   250
  A torment—ev'n mistook, as if a body
  Whose death were drowning, must needs therefore suffer it
  In scalding oil.

LIVIA   Sweet sir!

LEANTIO   As long as mine eye saw thee,
  I half enjoyed thee.

LIVIA   Sir?

LEANTIO   Canst thou forget
  The dear pains my love took, how it has watched   255
  Whole nights together in all weathers for thee,
  Yet stood in heart more merry than the tempests
  That sung about mine ears, like dangerous flatterers
  That can set all their mischiefs to sweet tunes;
  And then received thee from thy father's window   260
  Into these arms at midnight, when we embraced
  As if we had been statues only made for't,

To show art's life, so silent were our comforts;
And kissed as if our lips had grown together.
LIVIA
This makes me madder to enjoy him now.   265
LEANTIO
Canst thou forget all this? and better joys
That we met after this, which then new kisses
Took pride to praise?
LIVIA   I shall grow madder yet. Sir!
LEANTIO
This cannot be but of some close bawd's working.
Cry mercy, lady! what would you say to me?   270
My sorrow makes me so unmannerly,
So comfort bless me, I had quite forgot you.
LIVIA
Nothing, but ev'n in pity to that passion,
Would give your grief good counsel.
LEANTIO   Marry, and welcome,
                                                        lady;
It never could come better.
LIVIA   Then first, sir,   275
To make away all your good thoughts at once of her,
Know most assuredly she is a strumpet.
LEANTIO
Ha! most assuredly! Speak not a thing
So vilde so certainly; leave it more doubtful.
LIVIA
Then I must leave all truth, and spare my knowledge   280
A sin which I too lately found and wept for.
LEANTIO
Found you it?
LIVIA   Ay, with wet eyes.
LEANTIO   Oh perjurious friendship!
LIVIA
You missed your fortunes when you met with her, sir.
Young gentlemen that only love for beauty,
They love not wisely; such a marriage rather   285
Proves the destruction of affection:
It brings on want, and want's the key of whoredom.
I think y'had small means with her?
LEANTIO   Oh, not any, lady.
LIVIA
Alas, poor gentleman! What mean'st thou, sir,

279 *vilde* vile

Quite to undo thyself with thine own kind heart?   290
Thou art too good and pitiful to woman.
Marry sir, thank thy stars for this blest fortune
That rids the summer of thy youth so well
From many beggars, that had lain a-sunning
In thy beams only else, till thou hadst wasted   295
The whole days of thy life in heat and labour.
What would you say now to a creature found
As pitiful to you, and as it were
Ev'n sent on purpose from the whole sex general
To requite all that kindness you have shown to't?   300

LEANTIO
What's that, madam?

LIVIA   Nay, a gentlewoman,
And one able to reward good things; ay,
And bears a conscience to't. Couldst thou love such a one
That, blow all fortunes, would never see thee want?
Nay more, maintain thee to thine enemy's envy;   305
And shalt not spend a care for't, stir a thought,
Nor break a sleep—unless love's music waked thee,
No storm of fortune should. Look upon me,
And know that woman.

LEANTIO   Oh my life's wealth, Bianca!

LIVIA
Still with her name? will nothing wear it out?   310
That deep sigh went but for a strumpet, sir.

LEANTIO
It can go for no other that loves me.

LIVIA
He's vexed in mind. I came too soon to him;
Where's my discretion now, my skill, my judgement?
I'm cunning in all arts but my own love.   315
'Tis as unseasonable to tempt him now,
So soon, as a widow to be courted
Following her husband's corse, or to make bargain
By the grave-side, and take a young man there:
Her strange departure stands like a hearse yet   320
Before his eyes, which time will take down shortly.   *Exit*

304 *blow* hang (*O.E.D.* cites no such usage before 1835)

317–19 *widow . . . there.* As the Lady Anne was courted in *Richard III*
  (Act I scene ii).
320–21 *stands . . . shortly.* The hearse was originally a wooden structure
  erected over the coffin for a certain length of time. Before the Reforma-
  tion it carried candles; after, verses and epitaphs.

LEANTIO
　Is she my wife till death, yet no more mine?
　That's a hard measure. Then what's marriage good for?
　Methinks by right I should not now be living,
　And then 'twere all well. What a happiness　　　　325
　Had I been made of, had I never seen her!
　For nothing makes man's loss grievous to him
　But knowledge of the worth of what he loses:
　For what he never had, he never misses.
　She's gone for ever—utterly; there is　　　　　330
　As much redemption of a soul from hell
　As a fair woman's body from his palace.
　Why should my love last longer than her truth?
　What is there good in woman to be loved
　When only that which makes her so has left her?　　335
　I cannot love her now, but I must like
　Her sin and my own shame too, and be guilty
　Of law's breach with her, and mine own abusing;
　All which were monstrous. Then my safest course,
　For health of mind and body, is to turn　　　　340
　My heart and hate her, most extremely hate her!
　I have no other way. Those virtuous powers
　Which were chaste witnesses of both our troths
　Can witness she breaks first—and I'm rewarded
　With captainship o'th'fort! a place of credit,　　345
　I must confess, but poor; my factorship
　Shall not exchange means with't; he that died last in't,
　He was no drunkard, yet he died a beggar
　For all his thrift. Besides, the place not fits me:
　It suits my resolution, not my breeding.　　　　350

　　　　　　　　Enter LIVIA

LIVIA
　I have tried all ways I can, and have not power
　To keep from sight of him. How are you now, sir?
LEANTIO
　I feel a better ease, madam.
LIVIA　　　　　　　　　　　Thanks to blessedness!
　You will do well, I warrant you, fear it not, sir.
　Join but your own good will to't; he's not wise　　355
　That loves his pain or sickness, or grows fond
　Of a disease whose property is to vex him

330-31 *there ... hell.* Proverbial: 'There is no redemption from hell'
　　(Tilley, R 60).

And spitefully drink his blood up. Out upon't, sir,
Youth knows no greater loss. I pray let's walk, sir.
You never saw the beauty of my house yet,   360
Nor how abundantly fortune has blessed me
In worldly treasure; trust me, I have enough, sir,
To make my friend a rich man in my life,
A great man at my death—yourself will say so.
If you want anything and spare to speak,   365
Troth, I'll condemn you for a wilful man, sir.

LEANTIO
Why sure, this can be but the flattery of some dream.

LIVIA
Now by this kiss, my love, my soul and riches,
'Tis all true substance.
Come, you shall see my wealth, take what you list;   370
The gallanter you go, the more you please me.
I will allow you, too, your page and footman,
Your racehorses, or any various pleasure
Exercised youth delights in: but to me
Only, sir, wear your heart of constant stuff.   375
Do but you love enough, I'll give enough.

LEANTIO
Troth then, I'll love enough and take enough.

LIVIA
Then we are both pleased enough.   *Exeunt*

Act III, Scene iii

Enter GUARDIANO *and* ISABELLA *at one door, and the* WARD
and SORDIDO *at another*

GUARDIANO
Now nephew, here's the gentlewoman again.

WARD
Mass, here she's come again; mark her now, Sordido.

GUARDIANO
This is the maid my love and care has chose
Out for your wife, and so I tender her to you.
Yourself has been eye witness of some qualities   5
That speak a courtly breeding and are costly.
I bring you both to talk together now,
'Tis time you grew familiar in your tongues:

---

358 *drink ... up.* 'With sighs of love, that costs the fresh blood dear' (*A
    Midsummer Night's Dream*, III, ii, 97).

Tomorrow you join hands, and one ring ties you,
And one bed holds you; if you like the choice.　　　　10
Her father and her friends are i'th'next room
And stay to see the contract ere they part;
Therefore dispatch, good ward, be sweet and short.
Like her or like her not—there's but two ways;
And one your body, th'other your purse pays.　　　　15

WARD
I warrant you guardiner, I'll not stand all day thrumming,
But quickly shoot my bolt at your next coming.

GUARDIANO
Well said! Good fortune to your birding then.　　　[*Exit*]

WARD
I never missed mark yet.

SORDIDO
Troth I think, master, if the truth were known, you never　20
shot at any but the kitchen-wench, and that was a she-
woodcock, a mere innocent, that was oft lost and cried at
eight-and-twenty.

WARD
No more of that meat, Sordido, here's eggs o'th'spit now;
we must turn gingerly. Draw out the catalogue of all the　25
faults of women.

SORDIDO
How, all the faults! have you so little reason to think so much
paper will lie in my breeches? Why, ten carts will not carry
it, if you set down but the bawds. All the faults! pray let's
be content with a few of 'em; and if they were less, you　30
would find 'em enough, I warrant you. Look you, sir.

ISABELLA
But that I have th'advantage of the fool
As much as woman's heart can wish and joy at,
What an infernal torment 'twere to be

16 *thrumming* trifling (from *thrum* = waste end of weaving thread)
19–26 *I never . . . women* (as verse O)
22 *woodcock* simpleton (the bird is easily snared)
22 *innocent* half-wit
22 *cried* i.e. by the town-crier

9–10 *Tomorrow . . . you.* 'Through all Italy ingenerall, the espousall or
betrothinge with the Ring, is made privately, the bride being never
seene by the Bridegrome before that day, and that performed, they
lye together in bedd' (Moryson 4, p. 453).
24 *eggs o'th'spit.* Delicate business in hand. Proverbial: 'I have eggs on the
spit' (Tilley, E 86).

Thus bought and sold and turned and pried into; when alas   35
The worst bit is too good for him! And the comfort is,
H'as but a cater's place on't, and provides
All for another's table—yet how curious
The ass is, like some nice professor on't,
That buys up all the daintiest food i'th'markets   40
And seldom licks his lips after a taste on't.

SORDIDO
Now to her, now y'have scanned all her parts over.

WARD
But at what end shall I begin now, Sordido?

SORDIDO
Oh, ever at a woman's lip, while you live, sir; do you ask
that question?   45

WARD
Methinks, Sordido, sh'as but a crabbed face to begin with.

SORDIDO
A crabbed face? that will save money.

WARD
How, save money, Sordido?

SORDIDO
Ay sir; for having a crabbed face of her own, she'll eat the
less verjuice with her mutton—'twill save verjuice at year's   50
end, sir.

WARD
Nay, and your jests begin to be saucy once, I'll make you
eat your meat without mustard.

SORDIDO
And that in some kind is a punishment.

WARD
Gentlewoman, they say 'tis your pleasure to be my wife; and   55
you shall know shortly whether it be mine or no to be your
husband. And thereupon thus I first enter upon you.
[*Kisses her*] Oh most delicious scent! methinks it tasted as if a
man had stepped into a comfit-maker's shop to let a cart go
by, all the while I kissed her. It is reported, gentlewoman,   60
you'll run mad for me, if you have me not.

ISABELLA
I should be in great danger of my wits, sir,
For being so forward—should this ass kick backward now!

37 *cater's* caterer's
38 *curious* fastidious
43 *at what end* ed (at end O)
50 *verjuice* sauce made from crab-apples

WARD

Alas, poor soul. And is that hair your own?

ISABELLA

Mine own? yes sure, sir; I owe nothing for't.   65

WARD

'Tis a good hearing; I shall have the less to pay when I have
married you. Look, does her eyes stand well?

SORDIDO

They cannot stand better than in her head, I think; where
would you have them? and for her nose, 'tis of a very good
last.   70

WARD

I have known as good as that has not lasted a year, though.

SORDIDO

That's in the using of a thing; will not any strong bridge fall
down in time, if we do nothing but beat at the bottom? A
nose of buff would not last always, sir, especially if it came
into th'camp once.   75

WARD

But Sordido, how shall we do to make her laugh, that I may
see what teeth she has—for I'll not bate her a tooth, nor
take a black one into th'bargain.

SORDIDO

Why, do but you fall in talk with her; you cannot choose
but one time or other make her laugh, sir.   80

WARD

It shall go hard, but I will. Pray what qualities have you
beside singing and dancing? can you play at shuttlecock,
forsooth?

ISABELLA

Ay, and at stool-ball too, sir; I have great luck at it.

WARD

Why, can you catch a ball well?   85

ISABELLA

I have catched two in my lap at one game.

---

74 *buff* strong leather

---

72 *strong bridge*. The bridge of the nose was affected in syphilis (to which
  camp-followers were particularly prone).

84 *stool-ball*. A game resembling cricket, in which the wicket was a stool.
  The mad maid in *The Two Noble Kinsmen*, obsessed with 'the *way of
  flesh*', invites her wooer to play at 'stoole ball' (Nonesuch Shakespeare,
  Act V scene ii).

WARD

What, have you, woman? I must have you learn to play at
trap too, then y'are full and whole.

ISABELLA

Anything that you please to bring me up to I shall take
pains to practise.   90

WARD

'Twill not do, Sordido; we shall never get her mouth
opened wide enough.

SORDIDO

No sir? that's strange; then here's a trick for your learning.
    He yawns [ISABELLA *yawns too, but covers her mouth*]
Look now, look now! quick, quick there.

WARD

Pox of that scurvy mannerly trick with handkerchief; it   95
hindered me a little, but I am satisfied. When a fair woman
gapes and stops her mouth so, it shows like a cloth stopple
in a cream-pot. I have fair hope of her teeth now, Sordido.

SORDIDO

Why, then y'have all well, sir, for aught I see. She's right
and straight enough now, as she stands—they'll commonly   100
lie crooked, that's no matter; wise gamesters never find
fault with that, let 'em lie still so.

WARD

I'ld fain mark how she goes, and then I have all—for of all
creatures I cannot abide a splay-footed woman: she's an
unlucky thing to meet in a morning; her heels keep together 105
so, as if she were beginning an Irish dance still, and the
wriggling of her bum playing the tune to't. But I have
bethought a cleanly shift to find it: dab down as you see me,
and peep of one side when her back's toward you; I'll
show you the way.   110

SORDIDO

And you shall find me apt enough to peeping!
I have been one of them has seen mad sights
Under your scaffolds.

WARD   Will it please you walk, forsooth,

87–102 *What . . . so* (as verse O)

104–5 *splay-footed . . . morning*. A splay foot was a mark to know a witch by:
        The doubles of a hare, or, in a morning,
        Salutes from a splay-footed witch . . .
        Are not so boding mischief
                        (Ford, *The Broken Heart*, V, i, 12–16).

A turn or two by yourself? you are so pleasing to me,
I take delight to view you on both sides.　　115

ISABELLA
I shall be glad to fetch a walk to your love, sir;
'Twill get affection a good stomach, sir
—Which I had need have, to fall to such coarse victuals.
　　　　　　　　　　　　　[*She walks about*]

WARD
Now go thy ways for a clean-treading wench,
As ever man in modesty peeped under!　　120

SORDIDO
I see the sweetest sight to please my master!
Never went Frenchman righter upon ropes
Than she on Florentine rushes.

WARD　　　　　　　　　　'Tis enough, forsooth.

ISABELLA
And how do you like me now, sir?

WARD　　　　　　　　　　　　　'Faith, so well
I never mean to part with thee, sweetheart,　　125
Under some sixteen children, and all boys.

ISABELLA
You'll be at simple pains, if you prove kind,
And breed 'em all in your teeth.

WARD　　　　　　　　　　Nay, by my faith,
What serves your belly for? 'twould make my cheeks
Look like blown bagpipes.

　　　　　　　　　Enter GUARDIANO

GUARDIANO　　　　　　　How now, ward and nephew,　　130
Gentlewoman and niece! speak, is it so or not?

WARD
'Tis so; we are both agreed, sir.

GUARDIANO　　　　　　　　In to your kindred, then;
There's friends, and wine and music, waits to welcome you.

122 *ropes* tightropes
123 *rushes* the (Jacobean) carpet
128–30 *Nay . . . bagpipes* (as prose O)

127–8 *simple . . . teeth.* A sympathetic toothache is one of the most common
　　psychosomatic ailments of husbands whose wives are pregnant:
　　　　There beats not a more mutual pulse of passion
　　　　In a kind husband when his wife breeds child
　　　　Than in Martino; I ha' marked it ever:
　　　　He breeds all my pains in's teeth still
　　　　　　　　　　　　　　　　　(*The Widow*, III, iii, 142).
　　kind also carries its meaning of 'true to type'.

WARD
> Then I'll be drunk for joy.
SORDIDO   And I for company;
> I cannot break my nose in a better action.   *Exeunt* 135

Act IV, Scene i

Enter BIANCA *attended by two* LADIES

BIANCA
> How goes your watches, ladies; what's o'clock now?
1 LADY
> By mine, full nine.
2 LADY   By mine, a quarter past.
1 LADY
> I set mine by St Mark's.
2 LADY   St Antony's,
> They say, goes truer.
1 LADY   That's but your opinion, madam,
> Because you love a gentleman o'th'name.   5
2 LADY
> He's a true gentleman, then.
1 LADY   So may he be
> That comes to me tonight, for aught you know.
BIANCA
> I'll end this strife straight. I set mine by the sun;
> I love to set by th' best, one shall not then
> Be troubled to set often.
2 LADY   You do wisely in't.   10
BIANCA
> If I should set my watch as some girls do
> By ev'ry clock i'th'town, 'twould nev'r go true;

1–18 *How ... parish.* Apparently inconsequential, this chatter about
watches serves to define the new Bianca. The clock/woman comparison
is a stock one: 'A woman that is like a German clock, Still a-repairing,
ever out of frame, And never going aright' (*Love's Labour's Lost*,
III, i, 186–9). In this interlude the implied comparison is extended to
become a comment on fidelity—just as it is in Dekker's *The Honest
Whore, Part the Second*, where Infælice suspects her husband, Hippolito:

INFÆ   How works the day, my Lord (pray) by your watch?
HIP   Lest you cuffe me, Ile tell you presently:
>   I am neere two.
INFÆ   How, two? I am scarce at one.
HIP   One of us then goes false.
INFÆ   Then sure 'tis you,
>   Mine goes by heavens Diall (the Sunne) and it goes true
>   (III, i, 109–13).

And too much turning of the dial's point,
Or tamp'ring with the spring, might in small time
Spoil the whole work too. Here it wants of nine now.   15

1 LADY
It does indeed, forsooth; mine's nearest truth yet.

2 LADY
Yet I have found her lying with an advocate, which showed
Like two false clocks together in one parish.

BIANCA
So now I thank you ladies. I desire
Awhile to be alone.

1 LADY   And I am nobody,   20
Methinks, unless I have one or other with me;
'Faith, my desire and hers will nev'r be sisters.

                                        Exeunt LADIES

BIANCA
How strangely woman's fortune comes about!
This was the farthest way to come to me,
All would have judged, that knew me born in Venice   25
And there with many jealous eyes brought up,
That never thought they had me sure enough
But when they were upon me; yet my hap
To meet it here, so far off from my birthplace,
My friends or kindred. 'Tis not good, in sadness,   30
To keep a maid so strict in her young days.
Restraint breeds wand'ring thoughts, as many fasting days
A great desire to see flesh stirring again.
I'll nev'r use any girl of mine so strictly;
Howev'r they're kept, their fortunes find 'em out—   35
I see't in me. If they be got in court
I'll never forbid 'em the country; nor the court,
Though they be born i'th'country. They will come to't,

---

30 *in sadness* seriously

32-3 *fasting ... stirring*   since poor Fasting-Days
       Were not made reckoning on, the pampered flesh
       Has play'd the knave, maids have fuller bellies,
       Those meals that once were saved have stirr'd and leapt,
       And begot bastards, and they must be kept
                    (Middleton, *The Inner Temple Masque*, 135–9).
35 *their ... out*   would a woman stray
       She need not gad abroad to seek her sin,
       It would be brought home one way or another
                    (Middleton, *The Changeling*, III, iii, 224–6).

And fetch their falls a thousand mile about,
Where one would little think on't.   40

Enter LEANTIO

LEANTIO

I long to see how my despiser looks
Now she's come here to court; these are her lodgings!
She's simply now advanced! I took her out
Of no such window, I remember, first;
That was a great deal lower, and less carved.   45

BIANCA

How now? what silkworm's this, i'th'name of pride;
What, is it he?

LEANTIO   A bow i'th'ham to your greatness;
You must have now three legs, I take it, must you not?

BIANCA

Then I must take another, I shall want else
The service I should have; you have but two there.   50

LEANTIO

Y'are richly placed.

BIANCA   Methinks y'are wondrous brave, sir.

LEANTIO

A sumptuous lodging!

BIANCA   Y'have an excellent suit there.

LEANTIO

A chair of velvet!

BIANCA   Is your cloak lined through, sir?

LEANTIO

Y'are very stately here.

BIANCA   'Faith, something proud, sir.

LEANTIO

Stay, stay; let's see your cloth-of-silver slippers.   55

BIANCA

Who's your shoemaker? h'as made you a neat boot.

LEANTIO

Will you have a pair? the duke will lend you spurs.

BIANCA

Yes, when I ride.

LEANTIO   'Tis a brave life you lead.

BIANCA

I could nev'r see you in such good clothes
In my time.

---

39 *fetch . . . about* take a roundabout course   43 *simply* absolutely
48 *legs* bows
51 *brave* well-dressed

LEANTIO   In your time?
BIANCA   Sure I think, sir,   60
  We both thrive best asunder.
LEANTIO   Y'are a whore.
BIANCA
  Fear nothing, sir.
LEANTIO   An impudent, spiteful strumpet.
BIANCA
  Oh sir, you give me thanks for your captainship;
  I thought you had forgot all your good manners.
LEANTIO
  And to spite thee as much, look there, there read!   65
  Vex! gnaw! thou shalt find there I am not love-starved.
  The world was never yet so cold or pitiless
  But there was ever still more charity found out
  Than at one proud fool's door; and 'twere hard, 'faith,
  If I could not pass that. Read to thy shame, there—   70
  A cheerful and a beauteous benefactor too,
  As ev'r erected the good works of love.
BIANCA   Lady Livia!
  —Is't possible? Her worship was my pandress.
  She dote and send and give, and all to him;
  Why, here's a bawd plagued home! Y'are simply happy, sir,   75
  Yet I'll not envy you.
LEANTIO   No, court-saint, not thou!
  You keep some friend of a new fashion.
  There's no harm in your devil, he's a suckling;
  But he will breed teeth shortly, will he not?
BIANCA
  Take heed you play not then too long with him.   80
LEANTIO
  Yes, and the great one too. I shall find time
  To play a hot religious bout with some of you,
  And perhaps drive you and your course of sins
  To their eternal kennels. I speak softly now—
  'Tis manners in a noblewoman's lodgings,   85
  And I well know all my degrees of duty—
  But come I to your everlasting parting once,
  Thunder shall seem soft music to that tempest.

79 *breed teeth* cut his teeth
83 *course* pack
84 *kennels* lairs (*O.E.D.* 1b)
86 *know* ed (knew O)

BIANCA
'Twas said last week there would be change of weather
When the moon hung so; and belike you heard it.   90
LEANTIO
Why, here's sin made, and nev'r a conscience put to't,
A monster with all forehead and no eyes!
Why do I talk to thee of sense or virtue,
That art as dark as death? and as much madness
To set light before thee, as to lead blind folks   95
To see the monuments which they may smell as soon
As they behold—marry, oft-times their heads,
For want of light, may feel the hardness of 'em:
So shall thy blind pride my revenge and anger,
That canst not see it now; and it may fall   100
At such an hour when thou least see'st of all.
So to an ignorance darker than thy womb
I leave thy perjured soul. A plague will come!   *Exit*
BIANCA
Get you gone first, and then I fear no greater—
Nor thee will I fear long! I'll have this sauciness   105
Soon banished from these lodgings, and the rooms
Perfumed well after the corrupt air it leaves.
His breath has made me almost sick, in troth.
A poor base start-up! 'Life—because h'as got
Fair clothes by foul means, comes to rail and show 'em!   110

Enter the DUKE

DUKE
Who's that?
BIANCA   Cry you mercy, sir.
DUKE   Prithee, who's that?
BIANCA
The former thing, my lord, to whom you gave
The captainship; he eats his meat with grudging still.
DUKE
Still!
BIANCA He comes vaunting here of his new love
And the new clothes she gave him—Lady Livia;   115
Who but she now his mistress!
DUKE   Lady Livia?
Be sure of what you say.
BIANCA   He showed me her name, sir,
In perfumed paper—her vows, her letter—
With an intent to spite me: so his heart said,

92 *forehead* front, impudence

And his threats made it good; they were as spiteful　　120
As ever malice uttered; and as dangerous,
Should his hand follow the copy.
DUKE　　　　　　　　　　　　　But that must not.
Do not you vex your mind; prithee to bed, go.
All shall be well and quiet.
BIANCA　　　　　　　　　　I love peace, sir.
DUKE
And so do all that love; take you no care for't,　　125
It shall be still provided to your hand.　　*Exit* [BIANCA]
Who's near us there?

Enter MESSENGER

MESSENGER　　　　　　My lord?
DUKE　　　　　　　　　　　　Seek out Hippolito,
Brother to Lady Livia, with all speed.
MESSENGER
He was the last man I saw, my lord.　　　　　　*Exit*
DUKE　　　　　　　　　　　　Make haste.
He is a blood soon stirred; and as he's quick　　130
To apprehend a wrong, he's bold and sudden
In bringing forth a ruin. I know likewise
The reputation of his sister's honour's
As dear to him as life-blood to his heart;
Beside, I'll flatter him with a goodness to her　　135
Which I now thought on—but nev'r meant to practise
Because I know her base; and that wind drives him.
The ulcerous reputation feels the poise
Of lightest wrongs, as sores are vexed with flies.
He comes. Hippolito, welcome.

Enter HIPPOLITO

HIPPOLITO　　　　　　　My loved lord.　　140
DUKE
How does that lusty widow, thy kind sister?
Is she not sped yet of a second husband?
A bed-fellow she has, I ask not that;
I know she's sped of him.
HIPPOLITO　　　　　　Of him, my lord?

122　*copy* example in a copybook
131　*sudden* impetuous
138　*poise* weight (*O.E.D.* 1b)
142　*sped . . . of* furnished with

DUKE
    Yes, of a bed-fellow. Is the news so strange to you?   145
HIPPOLITO
    I hope 'tis so to all.
DUKE   I wish it were, sir,
    But 'tis confessed too fast. Her ignorant pleasures,
    Only by lust instructed, have received
    Into their services an impudent boaster,
    One that does raise his glory from her shame,   150
    And tells the midday sun what's done in darkness.
    Yet blinded with her appetite, wastes her wealth;
    Buys her disgraces at a dearer rate
    Than bounteous housekeepers purchase their honour.
    Nothing sads me so much, as that in love   155
    To thee and to thy blood, I had picked out
    A worthy match for her, the great Vincentio,
    High in our favour and in all men's thoughts.
HIPPOLITO
    Oh thou destruction of all happy fortunes,
    Unsated blood! Know you the name, my lord,   160
    Of her abuser?
DUKE   One Leantio.
HIPPOLITO
    He's a factor!
DUKE   He nev'r made so brave a voyage
    By his own talk.
HIPPOLITO   The poor old widow's son!
    I humbly take my leave.
DUKE   —I see 'tis done.
    Give her good counsel, make her see her error;   165
    I know she'll harken to you.
HIPPOLITO   Yes, my lord,
    I make no doubt—as I shall take the course
    Which she shall never know till it be acted;
    And when she wakes to honour, then she'll thank me for't.
    I'll imitate the pities of old surgeons   170
    To this lost limb, who ere they show their art
    Cast one asleep, then cut the diseased part:
    So out of love to her I pity most,
    She shall not feel him going till he's lost;
    Then she'll commend the cure.   *Exit*
DUKE   The great cure's past.   175
    I count this done already; his wrath's sure,
    And speaks an injury deep. Farewell, Leantio;
    This place will never hear thee murmur more.

Enter LORD CARDINAL, *attended*

Our noble brother, welcome!
CARDINAL   Set those lights down.
  Depart till you be called.   [*Exit* ATTENDANT]
DUKE   There's serious business   180
  Fixed in his look—nay, it inclines a little
  To the dark colour of a discontentment.
  Brother, what is't commands your eye so powerfully?
  Speak, you seem lost.
CARDINAL   The thing I look on seems so,
  To my eyes lost for ever.
DUKE   You look on me.   185
CARDINAL
  What a grief 'tis to a religious feeling
  To think a man should have a friend so goodly,
  So wise, so noble—nay, a duke, a brother;
  And all this certainly damned!
DUKE   How!
CARDINAL   'Tis no wonder,
  If your great sin can do't. Dare you look up,   190
  For thinking of a vengeance? dare you sleep,
  For fear of never waking but to death?
  And dedicate unto a strumpet's love
  The strength of your affections, zeal and health?
  Here you stand now: can you assure your pleasures   195
  You shall once more enjoy her—but once more?
  Alas, you cannot! What a misery 'tis, then,
  To be more certain of eternal death
  Than of a next embrace. Nay, shall I show you
  How more unfortunate you stand in sin,   200
  Than the low private man: all his offences,
  Like enclosed grounds, keep but about himself
  And seldom stretch beyond his own soul's bounds;
  And when a man grows miserable, 'tis some comfort
  When he's no further charged than with himself: 205
  'Tis a sweet ease to wretchedness. But, great man,
  Ev'ry sin thou commit'st shows like a flame
  Upon a mountain; 'tis seen far about,
  And with a big wind made of popular breath
  The sparkles fly through cities; here one takes,   210
  Another catches there, and in short time
  Waste all to cinders: but remember still,
  What burnt the valleys, first came from the hill.

201 *low* ed (love O)

Ev'ry offence draws his particular pain;
But 'tis example proves the great man's bane. 215
The sins of mean men lie like scattered parcels
Of an unperfect bill; but when such fall,
Then comes example, and that sums up all.
And this your reason grants: if men of good lives,
Who by their virtuous actions stir up others 220
To noble and religious imitation,
Receive the greater glory after death—
As sin must needs confess—what may they feel
In height of torments and in weight of vengeance;
Not only they themselves not doing well, 225
But sets a light up to show men to hell?

DUKE

If you have done, I have. No more, sweet brother.

CARDINAL

I know time spent in goodness is too tedious;
This had not been a moment's space in lust, now.
How dare you venture on eternal pain, 230
That cannot bear a minute's reprehension?
Methinks you should endure to hear that talked of
Which you so strive to suffer. Oh my brother!
What were you, if you were taken now?
My heart weeps blood to think on't; 'tis a work 235
Of infinite mercy you can never merit,
That yet you are not death struck—no, not yet . . .
I dare not stay you long, for fear you should not
Have time enough allowed you to repent in.
There's but this wall betwixt you and destruction 240
When y'are at strongest; and but poor thin clay.
Think upon't, brother! Can you come so near it
For a fair strumpet's love, and fall into
A torment that knows neither end nor bottom
For beauty but the deepness of a skin, 245
And that not of their own neither? Is she a thing
Whom sickness dare not visit, or age look on,
Or death resist? does the worm shun her grave?
If not (as your soul knows it) why should lust
Bring man to lasting pain, for rotten dust? 250

DUKE

Brother of spotless honour, let me weep
The first of my repentance in thy bosom,
And show the blest fruits of a thankful spirit;
And if I ere keep woman more unlawfully,
May I want penitence at my greatest need: 255

And wise men know there is no barren place
Threatens more famine, than a dearth in grace.
CARDINAL
Why, here's a conversion is at this time, brother,
Sung for a hymn in Heaven; and at this instant,
The powers of darkness groan, makes all hell sorry.   260
First, I praise Heaven; then in my work I glory.
Who's there attends without?

Enter SERVANTS

SERVANT   My lord?
CARDINAL
Take up those lights; there was a thicker darkness
When they came first. The peace of a fair soul
Keep with my noble brother.   *Exit* CARDINAL, *etc.*
DUKE   Joys be with you, sir.   265
She lies alone tonight for't; and must still,
Though it be hard to conquer. But I have vowed
Never to know her as a strumpet more,
And I must save my oath. If fury fail not,
Her husband dies tonight, or at the most   270
Lives not to see the morning spent tomorrow;
Then will I make her lawfully mine own,
Without this sin and horror. Now I'm chidden
For what I shall enjoy then unforbidden,
And I'll not freeze in stoves; 'tis but a while   275
Live like a hopeful bridegroom, chaste from flesh,
And pleasure then will seem new, fair and fresh.   *Exit*

Act IV, Scene ii

Enter HIPPOLITO

HIPPOLITO
The morning so far wasted, yet his baseness
So impudent? See if the very sun do not blush at him!
Dare he do thus much, and know me alive!
Put case one must be vicious—as I know myself
Monstrously guilty—there's a blind time made for't;   5
He might use only that, 'twere conscionable;
Art, silence, closeness, subtlety and darkness

275 *stoves* heated rooms
  4 *Put case* Assuming

---

259 *Sung . . . Heaven.* 'There is joy in the presence of the angels of God over
one sinner that repenteth' (*St Luke*, xv, 10).

Are fit for such a business: but there's no pity
To be bestowed on an apparent sinner,
An impudent daylight lecher! The great zeal   10
I bear to her advancement in this match
With Lord Vincentio, as the duke has wrought it,
To the perpetual honour of our house,
Puts fire into my blood, to purge the air
Of this corruption, fear it spread too far   15
And poison the whole hopes of this fair fortune.
I love her good so dearly, that no brother
Shall venture farther for a sister's glory
Than I for her preferment.

Enter LEANTIO and a PAGE

LEANTIO   Once again
I'll see that glist'ring whore shines like a serpent,   20
Now the court sun's upon her. Page!
PAGE   Anon sir!
LEANTIO
I'll go in state too; see the coach be ready.   [<i>Exit</i> PAGE]

I'll hurry away presently.
HIPPOLITO   Yes, you shall hurry,
And the devil after you; take that at setting forth!
                                    [<i>Strikes him</i>]
Now, and you'll draw, we are upon equal terms, sir.   25
Thou took'st advantage of my name in honour
Upon my sister; I nev'r saw the stroke
Come, till I found my reputation bleeding;
And therefore count it I no sin to valour
To serve thy lust so. Now we are of even hand,   30
Take your best course against me. You must die.
LEANTIO
How close sticks envy to man's happiness!
When I was poor, and little cared for life,
I had no such means offered me to die,
No man's wrath minded me. Slave, I turn this to thee,   35
To call thee to account for a wound lately
Of a base stamp upon me.
HIPPOLITO   'Twas most fit
For a base metal. Come and fetch one now,

9 <i>apparent</i> obvious
25 <i>and</i> if
38 <i>metal</i> with a pun on mettle

More noble, then; for I will use thee fairer
Than thou hast done thine own soul or our honour.   40
                              [*They fight*]
And there I think 'tis for thee.
VOICES *within*   Help, help! oh part 'em.
LEANTIO
False wife, I feel now th'hast paid heartily for me.
Rise, strumpet, by my fall! Thy lust may reign now;
My heart-string and the marriage-knot that tied thee
Breaks both together.
HIPPOLITO   There I heard the sound on't,   45
And never liked string better.

    Enter GUARDIANO, LIVIA, ISABELLA, WARD, *and* SORDIDO

LIVIA   'Tis my brother!
Are you hurt, sir?
HIPPOLITO   Not anything.
LIVIA   Blessed fortune!
Shift for thyself; what is he thou hast killed?
HIPPOLITO
Our honour's enemy.
GUARDIANO   Know you this man, lady?
LIVIA
Leantio! My love's joy! Wounds stick upon thee   50
As deadly as thy sins! art thou not hurt?
The devil take that fortune. And he dead!
Drop plagues into thy bowels without voice,
Secret and fearful. Run for officers!
Let him be apprehended with all speed,   55
For fear he 'scape away; lay hands on him,
We cannot be too sure. 'Tis wilful murder!
You do Heaven's vengeance and the law just service;
You know him not as I do—he's a villain,
As monstrous as a prodigy, and as dreadful.   60
HIPPOLITO
Will you but entertain a noble patience
Till you but hear the reason, worthy sister!
LIVIA
The reason! that's a jest hell falls a-laughing at!
Is there a reason found for the destruction
Of our more lawful loves? and was there none   65

40 *thine own soul* ed (thine soul O)
42 *paid* ed (praid O)
60 *prodigy* monster

To kill the black lust 'twixt thy niece and thee
That has kept close so long?

GUARDIANO   How's that, good madam?

LIVIA

Too true sir! There she stands, let her deny't;
The deed cries shortly in the midwife's arms,
Unless the parents' sins strike it still-born;   70
And if you be not deaf and ignorant,
You'll hear strange notes ere long. Look upon me, wench!
'Twas I betrayed thy honour subtilly to him
Under a false tale; it lights upon me now!
His arm has paid me home upon thy breast,   75
My sweet, beloved Leantio!

GUARDIANO   Was my judgement
And care in choice so dev'lishly abused,
So beyond-shamefully—all the world will grin at me!

WARD

Oh Sordido, Sordido, I'm damned, I'm damned!

SORDIDO

Damned! why, sir?

WARD   One of the wicked; dost not see't?   80
A cuckold, a plain reprobate cuckold!

SORDIDO

Nay, and you be damned for that, be of good cheer, sir—
y'have gallant company of all professions; I'll have a wife
next Sunday too, because I'll along with you myself.

WARD

That will be some comfort yet.   85

LIVIA

You, sir, that bear your load of injuries
As I of sorrows, lend me your grieved strength
To this sad burthen who, in life, wore actions
Flames were not nimbler. We will talk of things
May have the luck to break our hearts together.   90

GUARDIANO

I'll list to nothing but revenge and anger,
Whose counsels I will follow.

        Exeunt LIVIA *and* GUARDIANO [*carrying* LEANTIO'S *body*]

82-4 *Nay . . . myself* (as verse O)

83-4 *wife next Sunday*. When she would be wearing her best clothes and
    looking deceptively virtuous. 'Who will have a handsome wife let him
    choose her upon Saturday and not upon Sunday' (Tilley, W 378).

SORDIDO

A wife, quoth'a! Here's a sweet plum-tree of your guardiner's
grafting!

WARD

Nay, there's a worse name belongs to this fruit yet, and you   95
could hit on't; a more open one! For he that marries a
whore looks like a fellow bound all his lifetime to a medlar-
tree; and that's good stuff—'tis no sooner ripe but it looks
rotten; and so do some queans at nineteen. A pox on't, I
thought there was some knavery abroach, for something   100
stirred in her belly the first night I lay with her.

SORDIDO

What, what sir!

WARD

This is she brought up so courtly! can sing and dance—and
tumble too, methinks. I'll never marry wife again that has
so many qualities.   105

SORDIDO

Indeed, they are seldom good, master. For likely when
they are taught so many, they will have one trick more of
their own finding out. Well, give me a wench but with one
good quality, to lie with none but her husband, and that's
bringing-up enough for any woman breathing.   110

WARD

This was the fault when she was tendered to me; you never
looked to this.

SORDIDO

Alas, how would you have me see through a great farthingale,

---

100 *abroach* flowing

---

93 *plum-tree.* 'Yea, Madam Gabriela, are you such an old jerker? then
Hey ding a ding, up with your petticoats, have at your plum-tree'
(Nashe, *Have with You to Saffron-Walden* (ed. McKerrow, iii, 113)).

97–8 *medlar-tree.* Eaten when decayed to a soft brownish pulp, the medlar
(a species of pear) was often compared to the female genitals or,
indirectly, to whores: 'You'll be rotten ere you be half ripe, and that's
the right virtue of the medlar' (*As You Like It*, III, ii, 125).

103–4 *This . . . too.* Middleton seems to have mistrusted the 'extras' in a
girl's education; he describes a 'delicate drab' kept at 'White-friar's
nunnery':

some unthrifty gentleman's daughter . . . for so much she seemed
by her bringing up, though less by her casting down. Endued she
was, as we heard, with some good qualities . . . she had likewise the
gift of singing very deliciously . . .

(*Father Hubburd's Tales*, viii, 81).

sir! I cannot peep through a millstone, or in the going, to
see what's done i'th'bottom.   115

WARD

Her father praised her breast! sh'ad the voice, forsooth!
I marvell'd she sung so small, indeed, being no maid; now
I perceive there's a young chorister in her belly—this
breeds a singing in my head, I'm sure.

SORDIDO

'Tis but the tune of your wives' cinquepace danced in a   120
featherbed. 'Faith, go lie down, master—but take heed
your horns do not make holes in the pillowberes!—I would
not batter brows with him for a hogshead of angels; he
would prick my skull as full of holes as a scrivener's sand-
box.   *Exeunt* WARD *and* SORDIDO   125

ISABELLA

Was ever maid so cruelly beguiled
To the confusion of life, soul and honour,
All of one woman's murd'ring! I'ld fain bring
Her name no nearer to my blood than woman,
And 'tis too much of that. Oh shame and horror!   130
In that small distance from yon man to me
Lies sin enough to make a whole world perish.
'Tis time we parted, sir, and left the sight
Of one another; nothing can be worse
To hurt repentance—for our very eyes   135
Are far more poisonous to religion
Than basilisks to them. If any goodness
Rest in you, hope of comforts, fear of judgements,
My request is, I nev'r may see you more;
And so I turn me from you everlastingly,   140
So is my hope to miss you. But for her,
That durst so dally with a sin so dangerous,
And lay a snare so spitefully for my youth—
If the least means but favour my revenge,
That I may practise the like cruel cunning   145

114 *going* passage
116–9 *Her . . . sure* (as verse O)
122 *pillowberes* pillowcases
123 *angels* gold coins (varying in value between 6/8d and 10/-)
124–5 *sand-box* perforated box filled with sand, used for blotting
137 *basilisks* fabulous reptiles with fatal glances

120 *your wives'*. O's *wives* could be a misprint for *wife's*, but I take the *your*
as a contemptuous generalisation applicable to all wives, and not to
Isabella in particular.

Upon her life, as she has on mine honour,
I'll act it without pity.
HIPPOLITO   Here's a care
Of reputation and a sister's fortune
Sweetly rewarded by her! Would a silence,
As great as that which keeps among the graves,   150
Had everlastingly chained up her tongue.
My love to her has made mine miserable.

                Enter GUARDIANO *and* LIVIA

GUARDIANO
If you can but dissemble your heart's griefs now,
Be but a woman so far.
LIVIA   Peace! I'll strive, sir.
GUARDIANO
As I can wear my injuries in a smile.   155
Here's an occasion offered, that gives anger
Both liberty and safety to perform
Things worth the fire it holds, without the fear
Of danger or of law; for mischiefs acted
Under the privilege of a marriage-triumph   160
At the duke's hasty nuptials, will be thought
Things merely accidental, all's by chance,
Not got of their own natures.
LIVIA   I conceive you, sir,
Even to a longing for performance on't;
And here behold some fruits.
                [*Kneels before* HIPPOLITO *and* ISABELLA]
                              Forgive me both!   165
What I am now, returned to sense and judgement,
Is not the same rage and distraction
Presented lately to you; that rude form
Is gone for ever. I am now myself,
That speaks all peace and friendship; and these tears   170
Are the true springs of hearty, penitent sorrow
For those foul wrongs which my forgetful fury
Slandered your virtues with. This gentleman
Is well resolved now.
GUARDIANO   I was never otherways.
I knew, alas, 'twas but your anger spake it,   175
And I nev'r thought on't more.

162 *all's* all as

159–60 *mischiefs . . . triumph.* 'A mask is treason's licence: that build upon—
    'Tis murder's best face, when a vizard's on' (*The Revenger's Tragedy*,
    V, i, 176–7).

HIPPOLITO   Pray rise, good sister.

ISABELLA

Here's ev'n as sweet amends made for a wrong now
As one that gives a wound, and pays the surgeon—
All the smart's nothing, the great loss of blood,
Or time of hindrance! Well, I had a mother,   180
I can dissemble too. What wrongs have slipped
Through anger's ignorance, aunt, my heart forgives.

GUARDIANO

Why, this is tuneful now.

HIPPOLITO   And what I did, sister,
Was all for honour's cause, which time to come
Will approve to you.

LIVIA   Being awaked to goodness,   185
I understand so much, sir, and praise now
The fortune of your arm and of your safety;
For by his death y'have rid me of a sin
As costly as ev'r woman doted on.
'T has pleased the duke so well too that, behold sir,   190
H'as sent you here your pardon, which I kissed
With most affectionate comfort; when 'twas brought,
Then was my fit just past—it came so well, methought,
To glad my heart.

HIPPOLITO   I see his grace thinks on me.

LIVIA

There's no talk now but of the preparation   195
For the great marriage.

HIPPOLITO   Does he marry her, then?

LIVIA

With all speed, suddenly, as fast as cost
Can be laid on with many thousand hands.
This gentleman and I had once a purpose
To have honoured the first marriage of the duke   200
With an invention of his own; 'twas ready,
The pains well past, most of the charge bestowed on't—
Then came the death of your good mother, niece,
And turned the glory of it all to black.
'Tis a device would fit these times so well, too,   205
Art's treasury not better. If you'll join,
It shall be done; the cost shall all be mine.

---

183 *this is* ed (thus O)

180–81 *mother . . . too.* 'O that a boy should so keep cut with his mother,
and be given to dissembling' (*More Dissemblers Besides Women*, I, iv, 38–9).

HIPPOLITO
    Y'have my voice first: 'twill well approve my thankfulness
    For the duke's love and favour.
LIVIA   What say you, niece?
ISABELLA
    I am content to make one.
GUARDIANO   The plot's full, then;   210
    Your pages, madam, will make shift for cupids.
LIVIA
    That will they, sir.
GUARDIANO   You'll play your old part still?
LIVIA
    What is't? good troth, I have ev'n forgot it!
GUARDIANO
    Why, Juno Pronuba, the marriage goddess.
LIVIA
    'Tis right, indeed.
GUARDIANO   And you shall play the nymph   215
    That offers sacrifice to appease her wrath.
ISABELLA
    Sacrifice, good sir?
LIVIA   Must I be appeased, then?
GUARDIANO
    That's as you list yourself, as you see cause.
LIVIA
    Methinks 'twould show the more state in her deity
    To be incensed.
ISABELLA   'Twould—but my sacrifice   220
    Shall take a course to appease you, or I'll fail in't,
    And teach a sinful bawd to play a goddess.
GUARDIANO
    For our parts we'll not be ambitious, sir;
    Please you walk in and see the project drawn,
    Then take your choice.
HIPPOLITO   I weigh not, so I have one.   225
                   Exeunt [all except LIVIA]
LIVIA
    How much ado have I to restrain fury
    From breaking into curses! Oh how painful 'tis
    To keep great sorrow smothered! sure I think
    'Tis harder to dissemble grief than love.
    Leantio, here the weight of thy loss lies,   230
    Which nothing but destruction can suffice.   *Exit*

214 *Juno Pronuba.* In this one of her many aspects, Juno watched over the
    arrangement of marriages.

Act IV, Scene iii

Hoboys

Enter in great state the DUKE *and* BIANCA, *richly attired, with*
LORDS, CARDINALS, LADIES, *and other* ATTENDANTS. *They pass*
solemnly over. Enter LORD CARDINAL *in a rage, seeming to break*
off the ceremony

CARDINAL

Cease, cease! Religious honours done to sin
Disparage virtue's reverence, and will pull
Heaven's thunder upon Florence; holy ceremonies
Were made for sacred uses, not for sinful.
Are these the fruits of your repentance, brother?   5
Better it had been you had never sorrowed
Than to abuse the benefit, and return
To worse than where sin left you.
Vowed you then never to keep strumpet more,
And are you now so swift in your desires   10
To knit your honours and your life fast to her?
Is not sin sure enough to wretched man
But he must bind himself in chains to't?—Worse!
Must marriage, that immaculate robe of honour
That renders virtue glorious, fair and fruitful   15
To her great Master, be now made the garment
Of leprosy and foulness? is this penitence,
To sanctify hot lust? What is it otherways
Than worship done to devils? Is this the best
Amends that sin can make after her riots: 20
As if a drunkard, to appease Heaven's wrath,
Should offer up his surfeit for a sacrifice!
If that be comely, then lust's offerings are,
On wedlock's sacred altar.

DUKE   Here y'are bitter
Without cause, brother: what I vowed, I keep   25
As safe as you your conscience; and this needs not.
I taste more wrath in't than I do religion,
And envy more than goodness. The path now
I tread, is honest—leads to lawful love
Which virtue in her strictness would not check.   30
I vowed no more to keep a sensual woman:
'Tis done; I mean to make a lawful wife of her.

s.d. Hoboys Oboes (French *hautbois*)
23 *comely* decent

CARDINAL

He that taught you that craft,
Call him not master long, he will undo you.
Grow not too cunning for your soul, good brother.   35
Is it enough to use adulterous thefts,
And then take sanctuary in marriage?
I grant, so long as an offender keeps
Close in a privileged temple, his life's safe;
But if he ever venture to come out,   40
And so be taken, then he surely dies for't:
So now y'are safe; but when you leave this body,
Man's only privileged temple upon earth
In which the guilty soul takes sanctuary,
Then you'll perceive what wrongs chaste vows endure   45
When lust usurps the bed that should be pure.

BIANCA

Sir, I have read you over all this while
In silence, and I find great knowledge in you,
And severe learning; yet 'mongst all your virtues   50
I see not charity written, which some call
The first-born of religion; and I wonder
I cannot see't in yours. Believe it, sir,
There is no virtue can be sooner missed
Or later welcomed; it begins the rest,
And sets 'em all in order. Heaven and angels   55
Take great delight in a converted sinner:
Why should you, then, a servant and professor,
Differ so much from them? If ev'ry woman
That commits evil should be therefore kept
Back in desires of goodness, how should virtue   60
Be known and honoured? From a man that's blind
To take a burning taper, 'tis no wrong,
He never misses it; but to take light
From one that sees, that's injury and spite.
Pray, whether is religion better served: 65
When lives that are licentious are made honest,
Than when they still run through a sinful blood?
'Tis nothing virtue's temple to deface:
But build the ruins, there's a work of grace.

DUKE

I kiss thee for that spirit; thou hast praised thy wit   70
A modest way. On, on there!   *Hoboys*

CARDINAL   Lust is bold,
And will have vengeance speak, ere't be controlled.

            Exeunt

Act V, Scene i

Enter GUARDIANO *and* WARD

GUARDIANO
Speak, hast thou any sense of thy abuse? dost thou know
what wrong's done thee?

WARD
I were an ass else; I cannot wash my face but I am feeling
on't.

GUARDIANO
Here, take this caltrop, then; convey it secretly into the   5
place I showed you. Look you, sir, this is the trap-door to't.

WARD
I know't of old, uncle, since the last triumph—here rose up
a devil with one eye, I remember, with a company of
fireworks at's tail.

GUARDIANO
Prithee leave squibbing now; mark me and fail not—but   10
when thou hear'st me give a stamp, down with't; the villain's
caught then.

WARD
If I miss you, hang me; I love to catch a villain, and your
stamp shall go current, I warrant you. But how shall I rise
up and let him down too, all at one hole? That will be a   15
horrible puzzle. You know I have a part in't—I play
Slander.

GUARDIANO
True, but never make you ready for't.

WARD
No?—but my clothes are bought and all, and a foul fiend's
head with a long contumelious tongue i'th'chaps on't, a   20
very fit shape for Slander i'th'out-parishes.

GUARDIANO
It shall not come so far; thou understand'st it not.

WARD
Oh, oh?

1–6 *Speak . . . to't* (as verse O)
5 *caltrop* spiked instrument, used to stop horses
7 *triumph* pageant

---

21 *out-parishes.* Parishes outside the city boundaries (where the Morality
plays featuring such characters as Slander might still be acted).

GUARDIANO

He shall lie deep enough ere that time, and stick first upon
those.   25

WARD

Now I conceive you, guardiner.

GUARDIANO

Away; list to the privy stamp, that's all thy part.

WARD

Stamp my horns in a mortar if I miss you, and give the
powder in white wine to sick cuckolds—a very present
remedy for the headache.   *Exit* WARD   30

GUARDIANO

If this should any way miscarry now—
As, if the fool be nimble enough, 'tis certain—
The pages that present the swift-winged cupids
Are taught to hit him with their shafts of love,
Fitting his part, which I have cunningly poisoned.   35
He cannot 'scape my fury; and those ills
Will be laid all on fortune, not our wills—
That's all the sport on't! for who will imagine
That at the celebration of this night
Any mischance that haps can flow from spite?   *Exit*   40

Act V, Scene ii

Flourish. Enter above DUKE, BIANCA, LORD CARDINAL, FABRITIO,
and other CARDINALS, LORDS *and* LADIES *in state*

DUKE

Now our fair duchess, your delight shall witness
How y'are beloved and honoured: all the glories
Bestowed upon the gladness of this night
Are done for your bright sake.

BIANCA   I am the more
In debt, my lord, to loves and courtesies,   5
That offer up themselves so bounteously
To do me honoured grace, without my merit.

DUKE

A goodness set in greatness! how it sparkles
Afar off, like pure diamonds set in gold.
How perfect my desires were, might I witness   10
But a fair noble peace 'twixt your two spirits!
The reconcilement would be more sweet to me
Than longer life to him that fears to die.
Good sir!

CARDINAL   I profess peace, and am content.

DUKE
I'll see the seal upon't, and then 'tis firm.   15

CARDINAL
You shall have all you wish.   [*Kisses* BIANCA]

DUKE   I have all indeed now.

BIANCA
But I have made surer work; this shall not blind me.
He that begins so early to reprove,
Quickly rid him, or look for little love:
Beware a brother's envy—he's next heir too.   20
Cardinal, you die this night; the plot's laid surely:
In time of sports death may steal in securely.
Then 'tis least thought on:
For he that's most religious, holy friend,
Does not at all hours think upon his end;   25
He has his times of frailty, and his thoughts
Their transportations too, through flesh and blood,
For all his zeal, his learning, and his light,
As well as we poor souls that sin by night.

DUKE
What's this, Fabritio?

FABRITIO   Marry, my lord, the model   30
Of what's presented.

DUKE   Oh, we thank their loves.
Sweet duchess, take your seat; list to the argument.

Reads:
    There is a nymph that haunts the woods and springs
    In love with two at once, and they with her;
    Equal it runs; but to decide these things,   35
    The cause to mighty Juno they refer,
    She being the marriage-goddess. The two lovers,
    They offer sighs; the nymph, a sacrifice;
    All to please Juno, who by signs discovers
    How the event shall be. So that strife dies.   40
    Then springs a second; for the man refused
    Grows discontent, and out of love abused
    He raises Slander up, like a black fiend,
    To disgrace th'other, which pays him i'th'end.

BIANCA
In troth, my lord, a pretty, pleasing argument,   45
And fits th'occasion well: envy and slander

29 *we poor souls that sin* ed (we, poor soul that sin O)

Are things soon raised against two faithful lovers;
But comfort is, they are not long unrewarded.   *Music*

DUKE

This music shows they're upon entrance now.

BIANCA

Then enter all my wishes!   50

Enter HYMEN *in yellow,* GANYMEDE *in a blue robe powdered with stars, and* HEBE *in a white robe with golden stars, with covered cups in their hands. They dance a short dance, then bowing to the* DUKE *etc.,* HYMEN *speaks:*

HYMEN

     To thee, fair bride, Hymen offers up
     Of nuptial joys this the celestial cup;
     Taste it, and thou shalt ever find
     Love in thy bed, peace in thy mind.

BIANCA

We'll taste you, sure; 'twere pity to disgrace   55
So pretty a beginning.

DUKE   'Twas spoke nobly.

GANYMEDE

     Two cups of nectar have we begged from Jove:
     Hebe, give that to Innocence; I this to Love.

[HEBE *gives a cup to the* CARDINAL, GANYMEDE *one to the* DUKE; *both drink*]

     Take heed of stumbling more, look to your way;
     Remember still the Via Lactea.   60

HEBE

     Well Ganymede, you have more faults, though not so
        known;
     I spilled one cup, but you have filched many a one.

---

50 s.d. *Hymen* in yellow. Hymen, the god of marriage, is traditionally represented in yellow robes.

57 *Two . . . Jove.* Ganymede was cup-bearer to Jupiter.

59–60 *Take . . . Lactea.* Mulryne has found an explanation for this unusual connexion of Hebe with the Milky Way (*Via Lactea*):

    . . . *Hebe*, one which was *Jupiters* Cupbearer, on a tyme, stombled at a starre, and shedde the wyne or mylke, that was in the cuppe, which colloured that part of heaven to this daye, wherefore she was pout out of her office

      (William Fulke, *A goodly gallerye with a most pleasaunt prospect into the garden of natural contemplation* (1563), E 6ᵛ).

HYMEN

    No more, forbear for Hymen's sake;
    In love we met, and so let's parting take.   *Exeunt*

DUKE

    But soft! here's no such persons in the argument   65
    As these three, Hymen, Hebe, Ganymede;
    The actors that this model here discovers
    Are only four—Juno, a nymph, two lovers.

BIANCA

    This is some antemasque belike, my lord,
    To entertain time;—now my peace is perfect.   70
    Let sports come on apace; now is their time, my lord,
                               Music
    Hark you, you hear from 'em.

DUKE   The nymph indeed!

Enter two dressed like nymphs, bearing two tapers lighted; then
ISABELLA *dressed with flowers and garlands, bearing a censer with*
fire in it. They set the censer and tapers on Juno's altar with much
reverence, this ditty being sung in parts

                    Ditty

Juno, nuptial goddess, thou that rul'st o'er coupled
                                  bodies,
Ti'st man to woman, never to forsake her; thou only
                       powerful marriage-maker;
    Pity this amazed affection: 75
    I love both and both love me;
    Nor know I where to give rejection,
    My heart likes so equally,
    Till thou set'st right my peace of life,
    And with thy power conclude this strife.   80

ISABELLA

    Now with my thanks depart, you to the springs,
    I to these wells of love.   [*Exeunt the two* NYMPHS]

---

64 *parting take* ed (part O); a rhyme seems to be called for

---

69 *antemasque.* A brief interlude (often comic) introduced before the
masque proper; subsequent events show Bianca's responsibility for this
one.

72 s.d. Enter . . . ditty. Middleton's masque here is appropriate to the
action of the play, but it also bears close resemblance to the masque
in Act V of *The Two Noble Kinsmen.* The use of incense was common
enough; it was recommended by Bacon in his essay 'Of Masques and
Triumphs' as being especially pleasant in hot, steamy rooms.

                                       Thou sacred goddess,
         And queen of nuptials, daughter to great Saturn,
         Sister and wife to Jove, imperial Juno!
         Pity this passionate conflict in my breast,   85
         This tedious war 'twixt two affections;
         Crown me with victory, and my heart's at peace.

         Enter HIPPOLITO *and* GUARDIANO *like shepherds*

HIPPOLITO
         Make me that happy man, thou mighty goddess.
GUARDIANO
         But I live most in hope, if truest love
         Merit the greatest comfort.
ISABELLA   I love both   90
         With such an even and fair affection,
         I know not which to speak for, which to wish for,
         Till thou, great arbitress 'twixt lovers' hearts,
         By thy auspicious grace, design the man:
         Which pity I implore.
HIPPOLITO *and* GUARDIANO   We all implore it.   95
ISABELLA
         And after sighs, contrition's truest odours,
                                       LIVIA *descends like Juno*
         I offer to thy powerful deity
         This precious incense; may it ascend peacefully.
         —And if it keep true touch, my good aunt Juno,
         'Twill try your immortality ere't be long;   100
         I fear you'll never get so nigh Heaven again,
         When you're once down.
LIVIA   Though you and your affections
         Seem all as dark to our illustrious brightness
         As night's inheritance, hell, we pity you,
         And your requests are granted. You ask signs: 105
         They shall be given you; we'll be gracious to you.
         He of those twain which we determine for you,
         Love's arrows shall wound twice; the later wound
         Betokens love in age: for so are all
         Whose love continues firmly all their lifetime   110

         90–92 *I love . . . wish for.*
                 a husband I have pointed,
               But doe not know him, out of two, I should
               Choose one, and pray for his successe, but I
               Am guiltlesse of election of mine eyes. . . .
                              (*The Two Noble Kinsmen*, V, ii).

Twice wounded at their marriage, else affection
Dies when youth ends.—This savour overcomes me!
—Now for a sign of wealth and golden days,
Bright-eyed prosperity which all couples love,
Ay, and makes love—take that!

    [*Throws flaming gold upon* ISABELLA *who falls dead*]
                          Our brother Jove   115
Never denies us of his burning treasure
T'express bounty.

DUKE   She falls down upon't;
What's the conceit of that?

FABRITIO   As over-joyed, belike:
Too much prosperity overjoys us all,
And she has her lapful, it seems, my lord.   120

DUKE
This swerves a little from the argument, though:
Look you, my lords.

GUARDIANO
All's fast; now comes my part to toll him hither;
Then, with a stamp given, he's dispatched as cunningly.

[GUARDIANO *stamps on the floor; the trapdoor opens and he himself falls through it.* HIPPOLITO *bends over* ISABELLA'S *body*]

HIPPOLITO
Stark dead! Oh treachery—cruelly made away! how's that?   125

FABRITIO
Look, there's one of the lovers dropped away too.

DUKE
Why sure, this plot's drawn false; here's no such thing.

LIVIA
Oh, I am sick to th'death! let me down quickly.
This fume is deadly. Oh, 't has poisoned me!
My subtilty is sped; her art has quitted me.   130
My own ambition pulls me down to ruin.   [*dies*]

HIPPOLITO
Nay, then I kiss thy cold lips, and applaud
This thy revenge in death.

                     Cupids shoot [*at* HIPPOLITO]
FABRITIO   Look, Juno's down too!
What makes she there? her pride should keep aloft.

112 *savour* ed (favor O)
123 *toll* entice

She was wont to scorn the earth in other shows.   135
Methinks her peacocks' feathers are much pulled.

HIPPOLITO
Oh, death runs through my blood in a wild flame too!
Plague of those cupids! some lay hold on 'em.
Let 'em not 'scape, they have spoiled me; the shaft's deadly.

DUKE
I have lost myself in this quite.   140

HIPPOLITO
My great lords, we are all confounded.

DUKE   How!

HIPPOLITO
Dead; and, ay, worse.

FABRITIO   Dead? my girl dead? I hope
My sister Juno has not served me so.

HIPPOLITO
Lust and forgetfulness has been amongst us,
And we are brought to nothing. Some blest charity   145
Lend me the speeding pity of his sword
To quench this fire in blood! Leantio's death
Has brought all this upon us—now I taste it—
And made us lay plots to confound each other:
The event so proves it; and man's understanding   150
Is riper at his fall than all his lifetime.
She, in a madness for her lover's death,
Revealed a fearful lust in our near bloods,
For which I am punished dreadfully and unlooked for;
Proved her own ruin too: vengeance met vengeance   155
Like a set match: as if the plagues of sin
Had been agreed to meet here altogether.
But how her fawning partner fell, I reach not,
Unless caught by some springe of his own setting—
For on my pain, he never dreamed of dying;   160
The plot was all his own, and he had cunning
Enough to save himself: but 'tis the property
Of guilty deeds to draw your wise men downward.
Therefore the wonder ceases.—Oh this torment!

---

156 *plagues* ed (plague O)

---

136 *peacocks' feathers*. Juno is often represented as accompanied by peacocks.
151 *riper . . . fall*. Perhaps Middleton learned this from Webster, many of
    whose characters, in dying, look back upon their lives and comment
    on the 'shadow, or deep pit of darkness' that they lived in (*The Duchess
    of Malfi*, V, v, 100).

DUKE
  Our guard below there!

Enter a LORD *with a* GUARD

LORD   My lord?
HIPPOLITO   Run and meet death then,   165
  And cut off time and pain.   [*Runs on* GUARD'S *sword*]
LORD   Behold, my lord,
  H'as run his breast upon a weapon's point.
DUKE
  Upon the first night of our nuptial honours
  Destruction play her triumph, and great mischiefs
  Mask in expected pleasures! 'tis prodigious!   170
  They're things most fearfully ominous: I like 'em not.
  Remove these ruined bodies from our eyes.
                                [*The bodies are taken away*]
BIANCA
  Not yet? no change? when falls he to the earth?
LORD
  Please but your excellence to peruse that paper,
  Which is a brief confession from the heart   175
  Of him that fell first, ere his soul departed;
  And there the darkness of these deeds speaks plainly:
  'Tis the full scope, the manner and intent.
  His ward, that ignorantly let him down,
  Fear put to present flight at the voice of him.   180
BIANCA
  Nor yet?
DUKE   Read, read; for I am lost in sight and strength.
CARDINAL
  My noble brother!
BIANCA   Oh the curse of wretchedness!
  My deadly hand is fal'n upon my lord.
  Destruction take me to thee, give me way—
  The pains and plagues of a lost soul upon him   185
  That hinders me a moment!
DUKE
  My heart swells bigger yet; help here, break't ope!
  My breast flies open next.   [*dies*]
BIANCA   Oh, with the poison
  That was prepared for thee—thee, Cardinal!
  'Twas meant for thee!
CARDINAL   Poor prince!
BIANCA   Accursed error!   190
  Give me thy last breath, thou infected bosom,

And wrap two spirits in one poisoned vapour.
Thus, thus, reward thy murderer, and turn death
Into a parting kiss! My soul stands ready at my lips,
Ev'n vexed to stay one minute after thee.   195

CARDINAL
The greatest sorrow and astonishment
That ever struck the general peace of Florence
Dwells in this hour.

BIANCA   So . . . my desires are satisfied,
I feel death's power within me!
Thou hast prevailed in something, cursed poison,   200
Though thy chief force was spent in my lord's bosom.
But my deformity in spirit's more foul:
A blemished face best fits a leprous soul.
What make I here? these are all strangers to me,
Not known but by their malice, now th'art gone,   205
Nor do I seek their pities.

CARDINAL   Oh restrain
Her ignorant, wilful hand.

[BIANCA *seizes the poisoned cup and drinks from it*]

BIANCA   Now do; 'tis done.
Leantio, now I feel the breach of marriage
At my heart-breaking! Oh the deadly snares
That women set for women—without pity   210
Either to soul or honour! Learn by me
To know your foes. In this belief I die:
Like our own sex, we have no enemy.

LORD
See, my lord,
What shift sh'as made to be her own destruction.   215

BIANCA
Pride, greatness, honours, beauty, youth, ambition—
You must all down together; there's no help for't.
Yet this my gladness is, that I remove,
Tasting the same death in a cup of love.   [*dies*]

213 *no enemy* ed (no Enemy, no Enemy O)

---

203 *blemished face*. Possibly the poison she has kissed from the Duke's lips
has burned into Bianca's own; with this her first impulse after the
seduction is achieved (cf. II, ii, 425–7).

CARDINAL

   Sin, what thou art, these ruins show too piteously!   220
   Two kings on one throne cannot sit together
   But one must needs down, for his title's wrong:
   So where lust reigns, that prince cannot reign long.

                                   Exeunt

FINIS

Printed in Great Britain by
The Garden City Press Limited, Letchworth, Hertfordshire